Marian Approaches
to Synodality

Marian Approaches to Synodality

Josephine Lombardi

Foreword by
Sr. Nathalie Becquart, XMCJ

Paulist Press
New York / Mahwah, NJ

NOVALIS

Scripture quotations are from New Revised Standard Version Bible: Catholic Edition, copyright © 1989, 1993 National Council of the Churches of Christ in the United States of America. Used by permission. All rights reserved worldwide.

Cover image: *The Embrace of Elizabeth and the Virgin Mary*. St. George Church, Kurbinovo, North Macedonia, 1191. Courtesy Wikimedia Commons
Cover design by Sharyn Banks
Book design by Lynn Else

Copyright © 2024 by Josephine Lombardi

All rights reserved. No part of this publication may be reproduced, stored in a retrieval system, or transmitted in any form or by any means, electronic, mechanical, photocopying, recording, scanning, or otherwise, without either the prior written permission of the Publisher, or authorization through payment of the appropriate per-copy fee to the Copyright Clearance Center, Inc., www.copyright.com. Requests to the Publisher for permission should be addressed to the Permissions Department, Paulist Press, permissions@paulistpress.com.

Library of Congress Cataloging-in-Publication Data
Names: Lombardi, Josephine, author.
Title: Marian approaches to synodality / Josephine Lombardi.
Description: New York: Paulist Press, 2024. | Includes bibliographical references. | Summary: "This book shows how Mary provides an exemplar for women's leadership and the process of synodality through listening to, understanding, and accompanying the people of God"— Provided by publisher.
Identifiers: LCCN 2023036652 (print) | LCCN 2023036653 (ebook) | ISBN 9780809156702 (paperback) | ISBN 9780809188321 (e-book)
Subjects: LCSH: Mary, Blessed Virgin, Saint, and Christian union. | Church—Union.
Classification: LCC BX9.5.M37 L66 2024 (print) | LCC BX9.5.M37 (ebook) | DDC 262.001/1— dc23/eng/20240130
LC record available at https://lccn.loc.gov/2023036652
LC ebook record available at https://lccn.loc.gov/2023036653

ISBN 978-0-8091-5670-2 (paperback)
ISBN 978-0-8091-8832-1 (e-book)

Published by Paulist Press
997 Macarthur Boulevard
Mahwah, New Jersey 07430
www.paulistpress.com

Published in Canada by Novalis

Publishing Office
1 Eglinton Avenue East, Suite 800
Toronto, Ontario, Canada
M4P 3A1

Head Office
4475 Frontenac Street
Montréal, Québec, Canada
H2H 2S2
en.novalis.ca

Cataloguing in Publication is available from Library and Archives Canada.
ISBN: 978-2-89830-139-1

We acknowledge the support of the Government of Canada.

Printed and bound in the
United States of America

To my husband, Robert, and our four children,
Teresa, Eriberto, Aniello, and Beata

Contents

Foreword ix

Abbreviations xiii

Chapter 1. What Is Synodality? 1

Chapter 2. Mary: An Accompanying Witness 22

Chapter 3. The Church Listening: A Marian Approach 56

Chapter 4. The Church Understanding:
  A Marian Approach 90

Chapter 5. The Church Acting: A Marian Approach 112

Chapter 6. Mary: Our Model for Synodality 130

Notes 149

Foreword

Since October 2021, "the Church of God is convoked in Synod." For the first time in history, all the baptized have been called to take part in a synodal path titled "For a Synodal Church: Communion, Participation, Mission." As we are experiencing this journey together—a journey of prayer, mutual listening, and dialogue to discern the voice of the Holy Spirit—this theological, pedagogical, and insightful book on Mary as a model of synodality is a most welcome resource. It is an insightful support for the ongoing personal and communal synodal conversion we have been called to by God as Church in the third millennium. In fact, Josephine Lombardi has a unique way of combining a Marian perspective with a synodal vision rooted in all the main documents on synodality published recently, expressing the concrete experience of this 2021 to 2024 synod. Moreover, she brings her perspective as a woman, wife, and mother who is also a respected Canadian theologian and author. And doing so, she underlines how a better integration of the Marian principle can be a way to foster synodality in the daily life of the Church at all levels. That is to say, Marian synodality retrieves the common priesthood of all the baptized brought back by the Second Vatican Council's focus on our common vocation as children of God. Before any differences of

Marian Approaches to Synodality

gender, roles, vocations, and charisms, we all have equal dignity, and we are all called to sainthood.

Contributing to the promotion of women's participation in the church, she gives concrete guidelines to this call coming strongly from the youth at the Synod on Youth, reinforced by the Synod on the Amazon and getting louder through this synod. We can't be a synodal church without women, and the figure of Mary is an inspiration for discerning the ways to journey together as men and women in the Church and in society, as well expressed here in the Final Document of the Synod on Youth:

Women in a Synodal Church

148. A Church that seeks to live a synodal style cannot fail to reflect on the condition and role of women within it, and consequently in society more generally. Young men and women ask this question forcefully. The fruits of such reflection need to be implemented through a courageous change of culture and through change in daily pastoral practice. A sphere of particular importance in this regard is the female presence in ecclesial bodies at all levels, including positions of responsibility, as well as female participation in ecclesial decision-making processes, respecting the role of the ordained minister. This is a duty of justice, which draws inspiration both from the way Jesus related to men and women of his day, and from the importance of the role of certain female figures in the Bible, in the history of salvation and in the life of the Church.

In this line, we can truly draw inspiration from the figure of Mary to reflect on the role and vocation of women in the church and in the society, and to continue to find ways to journey together men and

Foreword

women discerning ways to involve more women in church leadership at all levels.

In my presentations on synodality I often say the "the family is the first school of synodality"; that's the fundamental place where we learn to journey together, to listen to each other, to dialogue, to love one another. From a Christian view, the family is a community of life and love called to reflect the life and communion of the Holy Trinity. The African Church has a beautiful expression that presents the Church as the family of God. So, we understand that the Holy Family and especially Mary have a lot to tell us about being a synodal church. The life of the Holy Family is a vibrant icon of an experience of synodality. In fact, a synodal church is first a listening church, and Mary is the great listener, the one who was shaped by her deep listening to the Word of God and who listened to the call of God to become the mother of the Son of God. She can guide us on the path of synodality in which we are learning how to say yes to the call of the Holy Spirit to discern how to be a missionary church at the service of the people in this world. With this book, we understand more how Mary inspires and helps us to say yes to synodality, that is, to say yes to the Holy Spirit, to communion, and to mission.

By her example, Mary is our model of listening. Despite her uncertainties and perplexities, Mary believed what she heard. She chose to open herself to the Holy Spirit, letting him fill her. Shaped by her listening to the Word, she let God take the initiative in her life. Through her yes, Mary let her whole life be transformed and overwhelmed by the surprises and wonders of the Holy Spirit. Mary's role in God's plan is indeed great, but she reminds us that each of us is indispensable and precious. God wants us to be masterpieces like Mary; our part is to give him our yes as she did. At Mary's school, we can learn how to listen together to God's voice calling us. This is the path

Marian Approaches to Synodality

of synodality: a Church of listening, where everyone has something to learn, where we listen to each other to hear what God has to say to us all. Mary is our first guide to a spirituality of listening that enables us to truly live the synodal nature of the Church. She knew how to preserve the things she received from God, pondering them in her heart (Luke 2:19). What a beautiful summary of the discernment to which we are all called! Mary let herself be guided by God's plans for her and for the whole world. Mary didn't think she knew everything beforehand. She put her trust in God, open to learning from him how to move forward step-by-step. In fact, even Mary had things to learn! She let herself be surprised by God, receptive to the gifts of the Holy Spirit. But what about us? How can we open the ears of our hearts like Mary, to listen to the Holy Spirit who reveals our deepest identity and helps us discover God's call for us?

Mary, you are God's way in our world, accompany your children on this synodal journey, and let your yes resound in our lives.

May we be renewed in our desire to answer the will of God asking us to become a synodal Church by the reading of this book, so that with a heart like Mary we can listen more and more deeply to the calls of the Holy Spirit for the Church in the third millennium.

Sr. Nathalie Becquart, XMCJ
Undersecretary for the General Secretariat of the Synod

Abbreviations

AA	*Apostolicam Actuositatem* [Decree on the Apostolate on the Laity], Vatican II, November 18, 1965
AAS	*Acta Apostolic Sedis* [Official Acts of the Holy See]
AG	*Ad Gentes Divinitus* [Decree on the Missionary Activity of the Church], Vatican II, December 7, 1965
AL	*Amoris Laetitia* [The Joy of Love], Pope Francis, March 19, 2016
CCC	*Catechism of the Catholic Church*
CCCB	Canadian Conference of Catholic Bishops
CDF	Congregation for the Doctrine of the Faith (now known as the Dicastery for the Congregation of the Faith)
CIC	*Codex Iuris Canonici*
DCS	*"Enlarge the Space of Your Tent" (Isa 54:2): Working Document for the Continental Stage,* Synod on Synodality, October 27, 2022
DV	*Dei Verbum* [Dogmatic Constitution on Divine Revelation], Vatican II, November 18, 1965
EC	*Episcopalis Communio* [Episcopal Communion], Pope Francis, September 15, 2018
EG	*Evangelii Gaudium* [The Joy of the Gospel], Pope Francis, November 24, 2013

Marian Approaches to Synodality

GS	*Gaudium et Spes* [Pastoral Constitution on the Church in the Modern World], Vatican II, December 7, 1965
IL	*Instrumentum Laboris* [Working Document for the Synod on Synodality], June 20, 2023
ITC	International Theological Commission
LG	*Lumen Gentium* [Dogmatic Constitution on the Church], Vatican II, November 21, 1964
MD	*Mulieris Dignitatem* [On the Dignity and Vocation of Women], Pope John Paul II, August 15, 1988
PD	Preparatory Document, *For a Synodal Church: Communion, Participation, and Mission*, September 7, 2021
PG	*Patrologia Graeca* (Collection of writings of Church Fathers in the Greek language)
PDV	*Pastores Dabo Vobis* [On the Formation of Priests in the Circumstances of the Present Day] Post-Synodal Apostolic Exhortation of John Paul II, 1992
Ratio	*Ratio Fundamentalis Institutionis Sacerdotalis* [The Gift of the Priestly Vocation], Congregation for the Clergy, 2016
RM	*Redemptoris Mater* [On the Blessed Virgin Mary in the Life of the Pilgrim Church], Pope John Paul II, March 25, 1987
UISG-USG	International Union of Superiors General
USCCB	United States Catholic Conference of Bishops

1
What Is Synodality?

Some of the best conversations take place while walking with a beloved friend or family member, especially when there is trust and intimacy, making us feel known and heard. As a mother of four adult children, I hope my children feel free to express their deepest desires, hurts, and joys with me. Some of my fondest memories include walking with my children to schools, parks, or other venues, listening to them chat about their experiences and delighting in their curiosity, especially when they wanted to learn something new about their environment.

Although I sense they trust me with their concerns, it troubles me to think they may be suffering in silence, afraid to approach or to be vulnerable with me. Sadly, some children may not approach their parents with their deepest vulnerabilities due to fear, not knowing how their parents may respond to their experiences, questions, or concerns. I desire that fear will never prevent my children from confiding in me for "perfect love casts out fear" (1 John 4:18). If there is fear in relationships, John writes, there can be no perfection in love because fear prevents the power of God's love, the Holy Spirit, from teaching, healing, and comforting. When there is fear in our love, we cannot

Marian Approaches to Synodality

reproduce the pattern of shared love revealed by the persons of the Blessed Trinity, because fear blocks the power of love.[1]

Unfortunately, fear has the power to render us irrational, feeding unchecked assumptions and fueling disconnection from others, thereby leading to greater division in families, communities, and the Church. Moreover, fear keeps us from recognizing the dignity and true identity of the other, as a beloved son or daughter of God, tempting us to focus on what divides and wounds instead.

As Church—the assembly of baptized believers, called, gathered, and sent to communicate God's love and desire to heal us—we are called to live in communion with one another and with the Blessed Trinity, our God.[2] We do this by living in relationship, building trust, and making God known to those who do not know God or have a distorted image of God in need of correction. Clearly, loving relationships are key to human flourishing; otherwise, people risk feeling rejected, scattered, and lost.[3] Recall Jesus's words when he said, "Whoever does not gather with me scatters" (Matt 12:30b). Like the parent-child dynamic, we cannot establish trust if people feel they cannot approach us with their experiences of vulnerability and pain. This can only happen if the image presented of the Church is one that invites, welcomes, accompanies, and listens. Among the many images of Church found in scripture and tradition,[4] the images of Church as Mother and Teacher come to mind when thinking about the current process of synodality.[5]

These models are fitting, especially when we think of the influence of mothers and teachers in families and in the greater community. I lost my mother twenty-two years ago and my father thirty-two years ago. Sadness overcomes me each time I have the desire to call my mother and share some good news with her, especially each time I want to call her to lament or process out loud. Not long ago, a friend of mine also lost both her parents. As we shared our common grief and sadness, I

What Is Synodality?

asked her, "What do you miss the most about your mother?" She replied, "I miss being known, and I miss sharing my life with her." The model Church as Mother reminds us of the need for connection and community. Similarly, the model Church as Teacher reminds us of the teachers we remember, especially their influence and impact on our lives.

Dr. Julie Hasson is the Nina B. Hollis Endowed Chair in Education at Florida Southern College. Her area of expertise is the qualitative research examining the influence and lasting impact teachers make on their students. Her research shows that we may not remember being taught certain lessons, but we remember being transformed at three levels: hearts, minds, and lives.[6] The Church, as the "universal sacrament of salvation" (*LG* 48) is called to this task of being an instrument of transformation, teaching and nurturing the faithful so that healing, sanctification, and conversion can take place. This process requires proper accompaniment and the art of listening to the joys and sorrows of God's people.

As the theme of the Sixteenth Ordinary General Assembly of the Synod of Bishops, synodality, the act of walking with the people of God and listening to their experiences of being members of Christ's body, marks a shift away from the previous synodal process of select representatives and scholars speaking on behalf of the people of God, allowing, instead, all Catholics the freedom to approach the hierarchy of the Church without fear or limitation. As we will see later in this chapter, previous synods focused on the study of a specific issue, concluding with some propositions and recommendations in response to the various issues addressed during the synodal consultations. Accordingly, the propositions informed the writing of papal post-synodal apostolic exhortations. The Church, in this most recent synodal process, while not ceasing to be Teacher, appears to present herself first as Mother, pausing the need to focus on a single doctrinal or pastoral issue and instead opening the process to

Marian Approaches to Synodality

all Catholics, ready to listen and understand, thereby reflecting on several key issues, and showing us how to walk with people. The Church, as "a good Mother," however, after having listened, responds as Teacher, showing us the way forward.[7]

The Church as Teacher, a model we have mastered for centuries, as expressed through the magisterium, and by extension through the teaching ministry of theologians and catechists, represents the handing on of revealed truths through the external curriculum of our faith, namely, catechesis and doctrine, including liturgical, pastoral, and legislative developments. Teaching, in which clergy, theologians, and catechists participate, is an extension of Christ's prophetic office. Church as Mother, however, participates in the handing on of the faith and also represents the handing on of the internal curriculum of our faith, for example, developing the interior life through human formation or character development, and building relationships through listening and dialogue.[8] On September 13, 2023, in a General Audience, Pope Francis affirmed the role of mothers in handing on the faith: "It's the moms who pass on the faith. The faith is passed on in dialect, that is, in the language of moms, that dialect moms know to speak with their children."[9] Church as Mother speaks to her children using language that is accessible, helping them to grow and to be more like Christ.

The internal curriculum, like the external curriculum, is part of the Church's evangelizing mission because it focuses on establishing relationships and helping people to trust and to listen to the people of God. Just as evangelization must precede catechesis, the internal curriculum must precede the external curriculum, meaning a trusting relationship with Church as Mother helps to pave the way for a trusting relationship with Church as Teacher. To be clear, men and women participate in both models of the Church. These two models are related because a good mother or parent teaches her children, and a good teacher nurtures her students. Hence, we need to know we are loved, heard, and seen before we can appreciate Church teaching—a key strategy in good pastoral care.

Although the Church is both Mother and Teacher, Church as Mother appears to be the model guiding the current process. Whereas previous synods addressed doctrinal and pastoral matters, the Synod on Synodality has another focus—listening to the experience of the people of God. Church as Mother invites the people of God to share their experiences of Church along with their lived experiences in family life. People are responding to the process in the same way a child comes to a parent with concerns and questions. However, a simple internet search reveals concerns about the process of synodality, showing some people are not sure what it is all about. It appears a model is needed, someone who can model synodality—Church as Mother for us. The Church identifies this model as Mary, the mother of Jesus. The Commission on Spirituality Sub-group writes:

> In Mary, we learn how to travel as a synodal Church. We learn to be at home in the world and to make a home for all those who are seeking home, a place of welcome and refuge, healing and salvation, a place of reconciliation, peace and the assurance of eternal life. This is a Church for which we long and need. At some point, we all become refugees seeking a homeland. With Mary, Mother of the Church, we learn how to make the Church, the Body of Christ, such a place, a people of living communion, participation and mission.[10]

Accordingly, inspired by one of the oldest icons of Mary known as the *hodegetria*, meaning "she who knows the way," the Commission on Spirituality Sub-group invokes Mary as a model of synodality under the title "Our Lady of the Way." She is the "one who accompanies the Church on its synodal journey."[11]

Marian Approaches to Synodality

Hence, Mary, who walked with God and listened, models for us what it means to listen and walk with God and God's people.

Mary, as a "pre-eminent and singular member of the Church" according to the teaching of the Second Vatican Council (1962–65), is a *"type* and outstanding *model* of faith and charity" for the Church (*LG* 53; emphasis mine). This means she models:

- how to live in *communion* with others and with God[12]
- how to *participate* in the divine life (2 Pet 1:4) and
- how to be a *missionary* disciple (Acts 1:13–16).

In other words, Mary models how to be Church. On August 4, 2023, during his visit to Fatima during World Youth Day 2023, Pope Francis referred to the Church as "the mother's house." We experience Mother Church, he said, "under the motherly gaze of Mary."[13] In Mary we see the fulfillment of the theme of the Synod on Synodality: "For a Synodal Church: Communion, Participation and Mission."[14] Having been identified as a model for the Church, and one who embodies "all the dimensions of the spirituality for synodality,"[15] it makes sense that her life witness be consulted as a model for synodality. Pope Francis encouraged all the faithful to entrust the work of the Synod on Synodality to Mary on May 31, 2023, the Feast of the Visitation.[16]

Indeed, the International Theological Commission (ITC), in their document on *Synodality in the Life and Mission of the Church*, affirmed this proposal, connecting synodality to evangelization, declaring that Mary teaches us "the beautiful, tender, and strong style of this new phase of evangelization" (121). This means walking with Mary, as Mother of the Church,[17] will show us how to walk with other members of our community of faith,

What Is Synodality?

evangelizing along the way. Accordingly, a Marian style of synodality will be the focus of this reflection, including an overview of synodality to launch the discussion.[18]

What Is a Synod?

On June 29, 2022, Pope Francis, reflecting on the purpose of the Synod on Synodality, called "us to become a Church that gets up, one that is not turned in on itself, but capable of pressing forward, leaving behind its own prisons and setting out to meet the world: a Church without chains and walls."[19] Synodality, as a process, invites us to be like Mary, recognizing the activity of the Holy Spirit in the world, encouraging us to *listen*, to *build communion*, to *participate*, and to foster a sense of *mission*, all key dimensions of the theme selected for the most recent Synod of Bishops.

The Preparatory Document, *For a Synodal Church: Communion, Participation, Mission*, marks the beginning of the synodal process of the Sixteenth Ordinary General Assembly of the Synod of Bishops, a process that opened in October of 2021 and continues past 2023 with two sessions, spaced one year apart: the first from October 4 to 29, 2023, and the second in October of 2024. The path of synodality, according to Pope Francis, is the path "which God expects of the Church of the third millennium."[20] Aware of the signs of the times, the Synod is taking place against the backdrop of "a global pandemic, local and international conflicts, growing impact of climate change, migration, various forms of injustice, racism, violence, persecution, and increasing inequalities across humanity, to name a few."[21] Additionally, the guidebook or *Vademecum* for the Synod on Synodality notes the internal struggles of the Church regarding the suffering "experienced by minors and vulnerable people" (1.1).

With the experiences of the people of God driving the process of the Synod, bishops will have the opportunity to hear the

Marian Approaches to Synodality

joys and sorrows of members of the global Church, inspiring them in their own discussions during the concluding part of the entire process. Fortunately for those who require more background regarding the meaning of synodality, we are helped by the work of scholars who have studied its meaning for the life of the Church.

In 2017, the ITC completed a study titled "Synodality in the Life and Mission of the Church." The study was inspired by the commitment made by Pope Francis at the commemoration of the fiftieth anniversary of the institution of the Synod of Bishops by Pope St. Paul VI.[22]

In 1965, as the Second Vatican Council was drawing to a close, Pope Paul VI established permanently a special council of bishops, "with the aim of providing for a continuance after the Council of the great abundance of benefits" seen flowing to the people of God throughout the Council, due mostly to the "close collaboration with bishops."[23] The Synod of Bishops is to "to be constituted in such a way that it is: a) a central ecclesiastical institution; b) representing the whole Catholic episcopate; c) of its nature perpetual; and d) as for structure, carrying out its function for a time and when called upon."[24] Consequently, he established by *motu proprio Apostolica Sollicitudo* on September 15, 1965, an apostolic letter launching the Synod of Bishops.

The general purpose of the Synod, according to Pope Paul VI, includes the promotion of a closer collaboration between the Supreme Pontiff and the bishops of the world; to gather "accurate and direct information" and "mutually useful information" that bears upon "the internal life of the Church"; to facilitate agreement on doctrinal matters and to recommend a suitable course of action.[25] Accordingly, the Synod of Bishops can meet in Ordinary General Session,[26] in Extraordinary Session,[27] and in Special Session.[28] Pope Francis, building on the teaching of Pope Paul VI, includes descriptions of these types of

What Is Synodality?

synodal assemblies in his 2018 Apostolic Constitution, *Episcopalis Communio*.[29]

Membership, consisting of episcopal representatives and consecrated persons, varies according to the type of session.[30] Nevertheless, Pope Paul VI, inspired by the principle of collegiality (*LG* 21–23), during the Sunday *Angelus* of September 22, 1974, defined the Synod of Bishops this way:

> It is an ecclesiastic institution, which, on interrogating the signs of the times and as well as trying to provide a deeper interpretation of divine designs and the constitution of the Catholic Church, we set up after Vatican Council II in order to foster the unity and cooperation of bishops around the world with the Holy See. It does this by means of a common study concerning the conditions of the Church and a joint solution on matters concerning His mission. It is neither a Council nor a Parliament but a special type of Synod.

Since 1967, there have been fifteen Ordinary General Assemblies of the Synod of Bishops.[31] Apart from synod hall discussions, synod members receive several documents: an outline of a proposed document (*lineamenta*), a working document (*instrumentum laboris*), reports before and after discussions, other preparatory documents, guidebooks, and finally, a document containing propositions put forward by the synod members, which have been used by popes to prepare post-synodal apostolic exhortations.

Although clergy and consecrated persons were the main drivers of the discussions that have taken place over the years, a key shift occurred during the Fourteenth General Assembly of the Synod of Bishops or the Synod on the Family, October 4 to 25, 2015, including the consultation of select lay faithful by way of questionnaires and other methods to gain awareness of

Marian Approaches to Synodality

the experience of the human family in today's context. Consequently, the input of lay faithful inspired the writing of a communiqué, dated February 17, 2016, issued by the Vatican Press Office, and prepared by Synod General Secretary, Cardinal Lorenzo Baldisseri, calling for a renewed understanding of the role of the lay faithful and their bishops. This understanding, writes Cardinal Baldisseri, "warrants considering not just the bishop of Rome and the episcopate in the synodal process, but also the lay faithful." Pope Francis, paying careful attention to voice of the lay faithful, sought to make this consultation permanent, including them in the synodal path going forward:

> The process of synodality, according to Pope Francis, reveals God's plan for us, namely, to walk together.[32] The document from the International Theological Commission (ITC) explains that the call to journey together is revealed in the deeper meaning of the term *synod*: "Synod" is an ancient and venerable word in the Tradition of the Church, whose meaning draws on the deepest themes of Revelation. Composed of a preposition (with) and the noun (path), it indicates the path along which the People of God walk together. Equally, it refers to the Lord Jesus, who presents Himself as "the way, the truth, and the life" (John 14:6) and to the fact that Christians, His followers, were originally called "followers of the Way" (cf. Acts 9:2; 19:9, 23; 22:4; 24:14, 22).[33]

Moreover, in ecclesiastical Greek, the term *synod* is used as a synonym for the ecclesial community; the ITC also gives the example of St. John Chrysostom using the noun *church* for *standing together*.[34]

In its study of the use of the term throughout the centuries, the ITC discovered the term has been applied to assemblies convoked at the diocesan, provincial, regional, patriarchal, or universal level.[35] This process of listening to the Word of God and pondering together the activity of the Holy Spirit accompanied the Church as doctrinal, liturgical, legislative, and pastoral issues emerged, demanding greater clarity, thereby developing our understanding of various teachings.

The Dogmatic Constitution on the Church, *Lumen Gentium*, a major teaching document of the Second Vatican Council, provided an opportunity to reconsider and "re-launch" the process of synodality.[36] Deep within its teaching is found the key theme of communion, used to describe the nature and mission of the Church. The Council, according to Dr. Moira McQueen, "used the terms 'council' and 'synod' somewhat interchangeably to describe its own proceedings, although 'council' was used more often and is more familiar to us."[37] Eventually, due to the influence of Pope Paul VI, the word *synod* was applied to a "representative body" meeting regularly, discussing a variety of topics.[38]

Pope Francis, in his address at the occasion of the fiftieth anniversary of the Synod of Bishops, stated, "From the beginning of my ministry as Bishop of Rome, I sought to enhance the Synod, which is one of the most precious legacies of the Second Vatican Council."[39] Informed by the input of the people of God, in communion with other bishops and experts, this council of bishops receives information and advice, allowing them to make decisions "when such power is conferred" upon them by the Roman Pontiff. Accordingly, Pope Francis continues, the lay faithful are invited to experience "the benefits of communion lived during the Council," highlighting the value and importance of consulting them in this process.[40] The ITC declares that "a synodal Church is a Church of participation and co-responsibility,"[41] the purpose of which is to "energize the life and evangelizing mission of the Church in union with and under the guidance of the Lord Jesus."[42]

Although there have been some developments involving more of the faithful in synodal consultations, the most recent synodal experience has taken the process of listening and responding to the experiences of the people of God to a new level.

Everyone is invited to share their experiences, participating in the process of the Synod, as well as the new policy of allowing official female representatives to vote,[43] including Sr. Nathalie Becquart, Undersecretary of the Vatican's General Secretariat of the Synod, who on March 31, 2023, in an interview with Global Sisters Report, revealed she will be voting at the Synod on Synodality.[44] Her comments were confirmed on April 26, 2023, when Pope Francis modified his 2018 Apostolic Constitution, *Episcopalis Communio*, to allow laymen and women to vote at the conclusion of the Synod in October of 2024.[45] Since the 1985 Synod, women have been invited to participate as experts and observers. This new development, however, builds on the previous step allowing a consecrated male participant to vote during the Synod on Youth.[46] Without doubt, the addition of female votes means greater participation and influence as the process of synodality embraces more voices. Accordingly, 464 individuals have been invited to participate, of which 81 are women. Voting delegates number 365, including some women.[47] This is a key development.

The Process of Synodality

As was previously noted, the current synodal process is anchored in three key ecclesial actions: communion, participation, and mission.[48] As vital pillars of a Synodal Church, they require input from all members of the Church, moving the process beyond a gathering of bishops. As stated in the *Vademecum*:

What Is Synodality?

One of the fruits of the Second Vatican Council was the institution of the Synod of Bishops. While the Synod of Bishops has taken place up until now as a gathering of bishops with and under the authority of the Pope, the Church increasingly realizes that synodality is the path for the entire people of God. Hence the Synodal process is no longer only an assembly of bishops but a journey for all the faithful, in which every local Church has an integral part to play. (1.3)

Although synodality does not exist without the authority of the bishops under the primacy of the pope (*Vademecum* 4.2), by asking key questions, including but not limited to, "How is journeying together happening today in your local Church? What steps does the Spirit invite us to take in order to grow in our journeying together?"[49] the bishops of the Church are anchoring the synodal process within the community of the faithful. Moreover, as a teaching and learning Church, the people of God is led by the guidance and inspiration of the Holy Spirit. Very clearly the *Vademecum* emphasizes listening to all the baptized:

> The entire People of God shares a common dignity and vocation through Baptism. All of us are called in virtue of our Baptism to be *active participants* in the life of the Church. In parishes, small Christian communities, lay movements, religious communities, and other forms of communion, women and men, young people and the elderly, we are all invited to listen to one another in order to hear the promptings of the Holy Spirit, who comes to guide our human efforts, breathing life and vitality into the Church and leading us into deeper communion for our mission in the world. (1:2; emphasis mine)

Marian Approaches to Synodality

The *Vademecum* refers to the *sensus fidelium* or the "sense of the faithful," a doctrine that was explicitly affirmed by the Second Vatican Council:

> The entire body of the faithful, anointed as they are by the Holy One, cannot err in matters of belief. They manifest this special property by means of the whole peoples' supernatural discernment in matters of faith when "from the Bishops down to the last of the lay faithful," they show universal agreement in matters of faith and morals. That discernment in matters of faith is aroused and sustained by the Spirit of truth. It is exercised under the guidance of the sacred teaching authority, in faithful and respectful obedience to which the people of God accepts that which is not just the word of men but truly the word of God. Through it, the people of God adheres unwaveringly to the faith given once and for all to the saints, penetrates it more deeply with right thinking, and applies it more fully in its life. (*LG* 12)

Affirming the influence of the *sensus fidelium*, Sr. Sarah Butler, a member of the ITC, credits the faithful in "keeping and transmitting the apostolic faith," including, by way of example, the development of doctrine surrounding Christology and Mariology.[50] The input of the faithful is key to this process, allowing the bishops of the Church an opportunity to listen to their concerns, including the tracking of their reception of a teaching. The key, however, is intimacy with the Holy Spirit, allowing the Spirit to lead us.

Unlike previous synods, the "objective of this Synodal Process is not to provide a temporary or one-time exposure of synodality, but rather to provide an opportunity for the entire people of God to discern together how to move forward on the

What Is Synodality?

path toward being a more synodal Church in the long-term" (*Vademecum* 1.3), Initially, reports Jos Moons, the process was designed to follow the previous format, that of a Synod of Bishops focusing on collegiality and inviting some experts to report on various issues.[51] Some past examples include the Thirteenth Ordinary General Assembly of the Synod of Bishops gathered in Rome from October 7 to 28, 2012, addressing the theme "The New Evangelization for the Transmission of the Christian Faith." The Fourteenth Ordinary General Assembly of the Synod of Bishops, or the Synod on the Family, took place from October 4 to 25, 2015. In 2018, the most recent Synod of Bishops studied the pastoral needs of young people.

Although these previous synods produced much fruit, the new process allowed the entire Church to participate in an initial phase of listening. This preliminary step was unique to the current Synod on Synodality, a synod consisting of four phases. The first of the four phases was a listening phase in the local Churches, adapted to local circumstances (*Vademecum* 1.5). This phase, among other things, was marked by an emphasis on discernment, cultural awareness, inclusion, dialogue, partnership, respect, and transparency, inviting the people of God to respond to questions prepared by the Synod of Bishops. The voice of the people of God was assisted by the collaboration with theologians—lay, ordained, and consecrated, helping them to express "the reality of the faith on the basis of lived experience" (*Vademecum* 1.3). Moreover, as stated in the *Vademecum*, the voices of those in the peripheries were encouraged:

> Special care should be taken to involve those persons who may risk being excluded: women, the handicapped, refugees, migrants, the elderly, people who live in poverty, Catholics who rarely or never practice their faith, etc. Creative means should also be found in order.to involve children and youth. (2.1)

Marian Approaches to Synodality

The second phase involved the Episcopal Conference and Synods of Oriental Churches, allowing synthesis of input and other deliberations to inform the preparation of a working document, *Instrumentum Laboris*, to assist with the third phase, the Continental Phase of the Synod. The working document was key to the discussions taking place for the seven continental meetings: Africa (SECAM), Oceania (FCBCO), Asia (FABC), the Middle East (CPCO), Latin America (CELAM), Europe (CCEE), and North America (USCCB and CCCB). These international meetings produced seven documents, serving as the basis for the second *Instrumentum Laboris*, released on June 20, 2023, which was used for the final and fourth phase of the Synod, the Assembly of the Synod of Bishops in October of 2023.[52]

Throughout this whole process, the presence and activity of the Holy Spirit is key. In a video message for the Plenary Assembly of the Pontifical Commission for Latin America, Pope Francis affirms the very present power of the Holy Spirit: "The Holy Spirit is not a force of the past. Rather, Pentecost is occurring in our time: the 'Great Unknown,' who has no image, is always contemporary and never ceases to accompany and console us."[53] He went on to say that the Holy Spirit is the "true protagonist of the synodal path." It is the Holy Spirit who animates the communion between "the *sensus fidei* of all of God's people, apostolic collegiality, and unity with the Successor of Peter."

To emphasize this key connection between the activity of the Holy Spirit and the participation of the faithful, my home diocese, the Diocese of Hamilton in Ontario, Canada, following the instruction provided in the main synodal documents, prepared a helpful brochure to assist the faithful in understanding what synodality is and what it is not. The main points are summarized in the table below.

What Is Synodality?

Table 1. What Is Synodality in the Catholic Church?	
What it is not:	· A democratic process to change the teachings of the Church. · A process to reach an already predetermined end result.
What it is:	· An opportunity for the whole Church to exercise their baptismal calling to be Priest, Prophet, and King in the Church today. · A way for the Church to hear the voice of the Holy Spirit who continues to guide the Church in every age.

Information Source: Diocese of Hamilton, Ontario, Canada.

In other words, as a listening Church, we recognize and acknowledge the input of the participants and allow for the Holy Spirit to affirm that which is true. Accordingly, the virtue of obedience, most perfectly embodied by Mary (*CCC* 148), must be acquired and present because Jesus obeyed God's will (Matt 26:39) and obedience, "must always be a Christian virtue and a characteristic of any Christian ecclesiology."[54]

Part of the reason synodality is so necessary is that it can refresh our ecclesiological vision for the Church. Discernment posits that the Holy Spirit is the arbiter, but the Church must be tasked with determining finally, to what the Spirit is or is not calling.[55]

The principle of synodality, then, according to the ITC, "is the action of the Spirit in communion of the Body of Christ and in the missionary journey of the people of God."[56] As a "Pilgrim Church" (*LG* chapter 7). we are "People of the Way."[57] The theme of the Synod, "For a Synodal Church: Communion, Participation, and Mission," shows God's people how to be "the Way," led

Marian Approaches to Synodality

by the Spirit, thereby showing us how to walk and stand with people.

The first dimension, communion, focuses on the unity of the Trinity, a pattern that is to be reproduced in the human family. This level of communion requires listening "to the Word of God, through the living Tradition of the Church, and grounding in the *sensus fidei* that we share" (*Vademecum* 1.4). Humility, a key virtue, will prepare hearts to listen and ponder the movement of the Spirit, encouraging us to participate in the process of synodality, therein helping us to understand the state of the human condition and our relationship with all of God's creation. As the second dimension, participation "is based on the fact that all the faithful are qualified and are called to serve one another through the gifts they have each received from the Holy Spirit" (*Vademecum* 1.4).

The Synod invites all members to pray, listen, analyze, dialogue, and discern, checking for the fruits of the Spirit, striving to know and to do God's will (*Vademecum* 1.4). This consultation will provide valuable input, encouraging the people of God to act according to promptings of the Holy Spirit. This means our context for synodality "begins in the presence of God, God's redemptive action in Christ and the outpouring of the Holy Spirit."[58] Moreover, the participation phase emphasizes the importance of the Eucharist, "the source and summit of the life of the Church" (*Sancrosanctum Concilium* 10).

The ITC's document on synodality linked participation in the life of the Church with the sacraments of Eucharist and Reconciliation.[59] Furthermore, it states:

> The Church's synodal path is shaped and nourished by the Eucharist. It is "the centre of the whole of Christian life for the Church both universal and local, as well as for each of the faithful individually." The source and summit of synodality are in the celebration of the

liturgy and in a unique way—in our full, conscious and active participation in the Eucharistic synaxis. Because of our communion with the Body and Blood of Christ, "We although there are many of us, are one single body, for we all share in the one loaf." (1 Cor 10:17)[60]

Similarly, the Preparatory Document presents the synodal way as the surest way to be the "universal sacrament of salvation,"[61] a sign of divine health and restoration, of vertical communion with God and horizontal communion with the whole human race.[62] As the purpose of our evangelizing efforts, the message of salvation is to be shared with everyone.[63] Hence, the universal salvific will of God drives all missionary and evangelizing efforts.[64] The third dimension of the synodal process, mission, reminds us of the purpose of the Church: to evangelize and make disciples of all nations. "Embarking upon a new chapter of evangelization,"[65] our evangelizing efforts will be marked by "a new ecclesial lifestyle" characterized by "words like conversion, openness, journeying, and the Holy Spirit."[66] Accordingly, these three dimensions, communion, participation, and mission, will inform the discussion taking place during the four phases. Although bishops are responsible for organizing the process involved in the four phases, input is not limited to episcopal collegiality. Consequently, the process needs accompanying witnesses, chief among them, Mary, the mother of Jesus.

As we will see in the next chapter, Mary embodies the dimensions found in the theme of the Synod: communion (Mary as model of the Church), participation (Mary using her gifts as a participant in the divine nature, 2 Peter 1:4), and mission (Mary helping Jesus as a participant in his salvific mission).

After contemplating these three key themes revealing the profound link between Mary and the Church, the focus of the next chapter, I use various biblical accounts including Mary, her

Marian Approaches to Synodality

words, and actions, to provide a framework for a Marian style of synodality. Chapter 3 will examine the account of the annunciation (Luke 1:26–38), showing how it models the Church listening, pondering, questioning with sincerity and trust, discerning, and accepting God's will. Using synodal input and Mary as a model, we will use this framework to examine some possible pathways for women in ministry, all grounded in our baptismal identity.

Chapter 4 will examine the account of the wedding at Cana (John 2:1–11), showing how it models the Church as it seeks to understand how observing where there is need and responding to vulnerability are keys to good accompaniment. Mary, modeling good human formation, shows us how to take notice of need and bring it to the attention of her son, Jesus, thereby showing us how Church as Mother provides input to Church as Teacher.

Chapter 5 will examine two accounts. Mary's visit with Elizabeth (Luke 1:39–56) will show how mutual recognition of dignity and anointing allows us to walk with others in their time of need, teaching us about empathy. John's account of the crucifixion (John 19:25–27), like the account of the visitation, models the Church acting like a mother, going to the peripheries to accompany the wounded, and standing with them in their time of vulnerability. Sometimes, we are called to walk forward and sometimes we are called to stand still. Here Mary models Church as the people of God walking and standing together.

The final chapter will explore recent developments in Mariology, showing how a complete doctrine on Mary may shed light on a complete understanding of the role of women in the Church. As we will see, including Mary in our synodal journey contributes to the conversation around women in the Church—a common issue raised in synodal discussions. States the Commission on Spirituality Sub-group,

What Is Synodality?

Mary, the mother of God, is always with us on the synodal path, for she is also "Mother of the Church" (*Mater Ecclesiae*)....Whenever we are feeling lost, confused, or hesitant about the way, we only have to look to her to point out the way.[67]

2

Mary

An Accompanying Witness

A magisterial document typically concludes with some sort of reference to Mary, often entrusting a special task to her maternal intercession. The ITC document on synodality is no exception:

> May Mary, Mother of God and Mother of the Church, who "joined the disciples in praying for the coming of the Holy Spirit (cf. Acts 1:14) and thus made possible the missionary outburst which took place at Pentecost" (*EG* 170), accompany the synodal pilgrimage of the People of God, pointing the way and *teaching us the beautiful, tender and strong style* of this new phase of evangelization.[1]

Similarly, in the companion synodal document, *Towards a Spirituality for Synodality*, Mary is presented as an accompanying witness, inviting us to share in her life journey:

> With her son, Mary knows all journeys that we each must make. She is truly "Our Lady of the Way." She,

too, has learned how to listen and respond to the Word that comes to her amid the routines of daily life, prayer, worship and family. She has learned how to speak the truth in humility, for she is also one of the *"anawim"*; how to proclaim the coming of God's Kingdom; how to serve it with unwavering faith and courage, not seeking her own path but only that which Christ walks.[2]

Mary listened to the Holy Spirit and pondered the meaning of her significant role in salvation history. If Mary is considered a model for the Church, a people standing together, it follows that some effort be put forward to understand what this means for the life of the Church. While there are many articles and books with more specialist reflections on Mariology and Ecclesiology, what follows is a contribution to the study of Mary and synodality. While three chapters will be dedicated to developing a Marian style of synodality, this chapter will explore three key themes regarding Mary's role in the life of the Church:

- Mary as model of the Church
- Mary and the Holy Spirit
- Mary and her son, Jesus

These key themes, I believe, show us how to be like Mary—striving for holiness as members of Christ's body, being receptive to the Holy Spirit, and remaining close to her son, Jesus, and by extension the Eucharist. Before we can discuss a Marian style of synodality, however, we need to deepen our understanding of what it means to be Marian.

As we will discover, being like Mary has "christological, pneumatological, ecclesiological and anthropological" implications.[3] Moreover, being like Mary means being inspired and filled with God's grace—God's "free and undeserved help that

Marian Approaches to Synodality

God gives us to respond to his call to become children of God," allowing us to participate in the divine nature or "the life of God" and to experience eternal life.[4] Pope Benedict XVI, emphasizing the importance of these implications, describes what it means for Mary to be "full of grace":

> Mary is a wholly open human being, one who has opened herself, entirely, one who has placed herself in God's hands boldly, limitlessly, and without fear for her own fate. It means she lives wholly by and in relation to God. She is a listener and a prayer, whose mind and soul are alive to the manifold ways in which the living God quietly calls her. She is the one who prays and stretches forth wholly to meet God; she is therefore a lover, who has the breadth and magnanimity of true love, but who has also its unerring powers of discernment and its readiness to suffer.[5]

In summary, as an instrument of God's love, Mary shows us how to be "wholly" open to God's will. Pope Benedict XVI, sharing this insight, explains Mary's life of grace is marked by the following characteristics and actions:

- Openness
- Humility
- Courage
- Obedience
- Magnanimous love
- Sincere discernment
- Dignified suffering
- Living by and in relation to God
- Listening to how God calls her
- Praying always to encounter God

In the discussion that follows, we will see how Mary models for us these characteristics and actions, especially understanding how they play out in relation to the Church, her intimacy with the Holy Spirit, and her intimacy with her son, Jesus.

Mary as Model of the Church: An *Ecclesio*-typical Approach

An *ecclesio*-typical approach to Mary emphasizes Mary as model and type of the Church (*LG* 53). As type, Mary "represents, foreshadows, and symbolizes" the Church.[6] As model, she reveals the way of being Church. In effect, Mary models **communion**, the nature and mission of the Church, with God and with God's people. In 1992, the CDF emphasized this connection between Mary and communion:

> The Blessed Virgin Mary is the model of ecclesial communion in faith, in charity and in union with Christ. *"Eternally present in the mystery of Christ,"* she is, in the midst of the Apostles, at the very heart of the Church at its birth and of the Church of all ages. Indeed, *"the Church was congregated in the upper part (of the Cenacle) with Mary, who was the Mother of Jesus, and with his brethren. We cannot therefore speak of the Church unless Mary, the mother of the Lord, is present there, with the Lord's brethren."*[7]

Hence, the members of the Body of Christ, the Church, are called to look to Mary as a fulfillment of God's plan for the Church, thereby seeking to reproduce the pattern we see in her. Pope Paul VI, following up on the Mariological developments of the Second Vatican Council, in 1974 prepared the apostolic exhortation, "For the Right Ordering and Development of Devotion to the

Blessed Virgin Mary," *Marialus Cultus*. Repeating the teaching of *Lumen Gentium*, Pope Paul VI proclaimed Mary as a mirror of the Church in its most authentic form.[8] Accordingly, this encouraged his successors and other Vatican departments to consider what it means to be Marian in the Church. The Congregation for the Doctrine of the Faith (CDF), for example, revisited this idea that Mary is the "mirror of the Church":

> In this regard, the figure of Mary constitutes the fundamental reference in the Church. One could say metaphorically that Mary is a mirror placed before the Church, in which the Church is invited to recognize her own identity as well as the dispositions of the heart, the attitudes and the actions which God expects from her.
>
> The existence of Mary is an invitation to the Church to root her very being in listening and receiving the Word of God, because faith is not so much the search for God on the part of human beings, as the recognition by men and women that God comes to us; he visits us and speaks to us.[9]

Moreover, the CDF emphasized her "disposition of listening, welcoming, humility, faithfulness, praise and waiting."[10] These dispositions, the CDF says, are rooted in Christ and "become the vocation of every baptized Christian."[11] Overall, to be Marian, among other things, involves cultivating a deep interior life or intimacy with God. Only then can we be fruitful like Mary. Hence, it would be helpful to understand how the Church lives out her fruitfulness.

Petrine and Marian Dimensions

The Church expresses herself through Petrine and Marian dimensions or principles.[12] The Petrine dimension can be understood as the service of the pope and the bishops "oriented to the building up and maintaining of the Church's life of faith, the living of the Christian life in communion and charity, and the unity of the Church."[13] Notwithstanding the activity of the pope and bishops, there are many qualified laypersons, including consecrated persons, who support the expression of the Petrine dimension: catechists, theologians, and canon lawyers, to name a few examples.

The Marian dimension, however, as a key ecclesiological principle, includes all members of the Church, the Body of Christ, including those who participate in the Petrine dimension. Living out the Marian dimension involves reproducing the pattern we see in Mary, whereby the Petrine dimension, inspired by the Holy Spirit, becomes more receptive and fruitful in its activity. According to Pope St. John Paul II, the Petrine "has no other purpose except to form the Church in line with the ideal of sanctity already programmed and prefigured in Mary."[14]

In Mary, then, we see the fulfillment of the four marks or essential characteristics of the Church.

Table 2. The Catholic Church and Mary: Essential Characteristics	
The Catholic Church	**Mary**
One	In unity/communion/union with God (Luke 1:38)
Holy	Partaker of the divine nature (2 Pet 1:4)
Catholic	Mother of the Church[i] (John 19:27)
Apostolic	Queen of the Apostles[ii] (Acts 1:13-14)

---

   i. Pope Paul VI declared Mary "Mother of the Church" in 1964.

   ii. The title "Queen of the Apostles" first appeared in various versions of the Litany of Loreto between the twelfth and fourteenth centuries. A feast day was approved in 1890. See Johann Roten, "Mary, Queen of the Apostles," https://udayton.edu/imri/mary/q/queen-of-apostles.php.

Marian Approaches to Synodality

Mary's maternal care for the Church has inspired her members to think more closely about what it means to be fruitful—to bring Christ into the world. Consequently, this study stimulated more interest in the feminine dimension of the Church, including the role of women in the Church.[15]

Reflecting on Mary's witness, Pope Francis in *Evangelii Gaudium*, challenges us to embrace a "Marian style" of ministry (104). Commenting on the role of women in the Church, on November 1, 2016, during an in-flight interview, Pope Francis seized the opportunity to emphasize the gifts of women and the Marian dimension of the Church, thereby affirming the connection between the Marian and the feminine, revealing a receptivity to the promptings of the Holy Spirit. He said, "There is no church without the feminine dimension,"[16] and he went on to say that Mary precedes all others. Moreover, in *Evangelii Gaudium* 39, he declared Mary to be "more important than the bishops." Similarly, in an interview with Vittorio Messori, Cardinal Joseph Ratzinger challenged Christians to see, as was affirmed by the Second Vatican Council, Mary as "figure, image and model of the Church," shielding against "a solely masculinized model."[17] Elsewhere, commenting on Mary as "type" of the Church, Ratzinger writes:

> (The) type remains true to its meaning only when the noninterchangeable personal figure of Mary becomes transparent to the personal form of the Church herself. Only the Marian dimension secures the place of affectivity in faith and thus ensures a fully human correspondence to the reality of the incarnate *Logos*.[18]

Inspired by an *Ecclesio*-typical Mariology,[19] Cardinal Ratzinger lamented the thought of a theology or ecclesiology that no longer had a place for Mary.[20] Emphasizing her humility,

Mary

receptivity, and obedience to God, she is, he says, "an example to which every Christian—man and woman—can and should look."[21] Moreover, John Paul II, aware of the risk identified by Cardinal Ratzinger and inspired by the ecclesiology of Han Urs von Balthasar,[22] had the courage to declare that the Marian dimension of the Church "precedes the Petrine,"[23] meaning "to be Petrine and to be Church require a fundamental understanding of what it means to be Marian."[24] Although the Church is "both Marian and Apostolic-Petrine," Mary represents the Church in its perfected state because she "precedes everyone on the path to holiness."[25] This implies the Marian dimension prevents the Petrine dimension from slipping into clericalism. Accordingly, the focus becomes service, not power.

In a letter addressed to the President of the Pontifical Commission for Latin America, Pope Francis decried clericalism, stating:

> (it) not only nullifies the character of Christians, but also tends to diminish and undervalue the baptismal grace that the Holy Spirit has placed in the heart of our people. Clericalism leads to homologization of the laity; treating the laity as 'representative' limits the diverse initiatives and efforts and, dare I say, the necessary boldness to enable the Good News of the Gospel to be brought to all areas of the social and above all political spheres. Clericalism, far from giving impetus to various contributions and proposals, gradually extinguishes the prophetic flame to which the entire Church is called to bear witness in the heart of her peoples. Clericalism forgets that the visibility and sacramentality of the Church belong to all the People of God, not only to the few chosen and enlightened.[26]

Marian Approaches to Synodality

The Marian dimension, as a key foundational ecclesiological principle, represents a response to clericalism, emphasizing the baptismal dignity of all members of the Church, the desire for holiness, and receptivity to the divine.[27] The greater presence of women, says Margaret Harper McCarthy, "could be a humanizing force, correcting the tendencies toward bureaucratic clericalism and careerism," reminding the Petrine dimension "that it owes itself to something other than itself, and that it is in *her* service."[28] Pope Francis, along with other representatives who had gathered for a symposium on the "Priesthood in the 21st Century," affirmed this point when catechesis on the baptismal priesthood was proposed as a way of combatting clericalism.[29] Knowing the deeper meaning of our baptism, then, confirms our **mission** in the Church, wherein the lay faithful are encouraged to **participate** and use their gifts, a key theme of the synod on synodality. Consequently, the collaboration and witness of the baptized inspire those who serve through Petrine dimension to be Marian in their mission. This means members of the hierarchy must cultivate certain virtues, including a deep interior life, humility, receptivity, and obedience, before they can teach, sanctify, and govern the people of God.

Like Mary, they are expected to model horizontal **communion**, that is communion with their neighbors, and vertical communion—communion with God. Just as all men and women are "formed in the likeness of Christ" (*LG* 7), all men and women are called to be Marian, too. It makes sense that the more we acquire certain Marian virtues, the more Christ is formed in us (*LG* 7). Nevertheless, this challenge is sometimes forgotten as one criticism of this approach, that of distinguishing between the Petrine and the Marian, is the risk of creating a separation, whereby the use of stereotypes is encouraged when it comes to men and women in the Church, namely, women are to be the nurturers (Marian) and only men can have authority (Petrine).[30]

Mary

Hopefully, we can come to understand the dynamic between the Petrine and the Marian dimensions with greater clarity by encouraging greater collaboration when it comes to members of the Church, lay, including consecrated persons, and clergy, teaching and nurturing her members. We will circle back to this possibility in the next and concluding chapters. Nonetheless, the pattern we see in Mary's presence and response to the divine is to be reproduced in any Christian, male or female, seeking to be more like Christ. Hence, modeling Mary is key to fruitful servant leadership.

In an address to the prelates of the Roman curia, Pope St. John Paul II, emphasizing the importance of modeling Mary, shared some thoughts on how the Church is Marian and Petrine:

> This Marian profile is also—even perhaps more so—fundamental and characteristic for the Church as is the apostolic and Petrine profile to which it is profoundly united....The Marian dimension of the Church is antecedent to that of the Petrine, without being in any way divided from it or being less complementary. Mary Immaculate precedes all others, including obviously Peter himself and the Apostles. This is so, not only because Peter and the Apostles, being born of the human race under the burden of sin, form part of the Church which is "holy from out of sinners," but also because their triple function has no other purpose except to form the Church in line with the ideal of sanctity already programmed and prefigured in Mary.[31]

The link between the Marian and Petrine dimensions, according to Pope St. John Paul II, is "profound and complementary."[32] This link, it seems, connects to two ecclesiological models,

Marian Approaches to Synodality

already addressed in the first chapter, that of Church as Mother and Teacher:

> Mother and Teacher of all nations—such is the Catholic Church in the mind of Her founder, Jesus Christ; to hold the world in an embrace of love, that men, in every age, should find in her their own completeness in a higher order of living, and their ultimate salvation. She is "the pillar and ground of the truth." To her was entrusted by her holy Founder the twofold task of giving life to her children and of teaching them and guiding them—both as individuals and as nations—with maternal care (Pope John XXIII, *Mater et Magistra* 1).

Monica Migliorino Miller in her book *The Authority of Women in the Catholic Church* describes the Church as a "school in divine life" where Mother Church admonishes and teaches the people of God with authority.[33] Nevertheless, as Miller suggests, the Church as Mother does more than teach and admonish her children; a Marian Church teaches and parents with authority and mercy. Mary, according to the Federation of Asian Bishops' Conferences, in their Final Document of the Asian Continental Assembly on Synodality, shows the Church how to be a "good mother."[34] Communicating God's tenderness, the Church is to reveal what it means to be Marian in the world today.

Following the teaching of the Second Vatican Council, that Mary is a model of the Church (*LG* 53), we are given a sneak preview of the Church in its perfected state, showing us the way forward into the mystery of Christ and his Church. Pope Paul VI, aware of this mystery, once remarked that knowledge "of the true Catholic doctrine regarding the Blessed Virgin Mary will always be key to the exact understanding of Christ and of the Church."[35] Mary, the Mother of the Church, reveals fresh insights into Church as Mother and Teacher. To understand this vision of the Church, more reflection on Mary as model of the Church is necessary.[36]

Pope Francis, commenting on the evangelizing mission of the Church, proposes that the model of Church as Mother shows the Church's "maternal side, her motherly face to a humanity that is wounded. She does not wait for the wounded to knock on her doors, she looks for them on the streets, she gathers them in, she embraces them, she takes care of them, she makes them feel loved."[37] This Marian vision captures what Francis calls "the Logic of Pastoral Mercy" (*Amoris Laetitia* 308).

In an earlier work, I explored the impact of the Marian dimension on the correct understanding of how the Church is called to be merciful and just, two expressions of God's love.[38] I argued that Pope Francis's "program of life,"[39] rooted in the mercy of God, is deeply Marian, reconciling the perceived tension between mercy and justice.

Mercy and Justice

To follow Mary's example on the synodal path, it is helpful to understand the way of justice and the way of mercy, two expressions of the one love of God. Using an approach used in legal contexts, that of "therapeutic jurisprudence"—an expression coined by two American law professors, David Wexler and Bruce Winnock—I showed how this multidisciplinary field of study offers a holistic approach to handling legal cases, thereby considering "the behavioral sciences and the desire to heal victims and perpetrators of crime. In other words, it is an approach that sees mercy and justice leading to healing and restoration of all those hurt by crime. It is justice informed by mercy."[40] In continuity with his predecessors, Pope Francis appears to support

Marian Approaches to Synodality

this approach by affirming the healing power of mercy, especially when it comes to synodality and collegiality.

Although Cardinals Mario Grech, Cardinal Secretary General of the Synod, and Jean Claude Hollerich, General Relator of the Synod, in their letter to diocesan and eparchial bishops, dated January 26, 2023, declare "there is no exercise of episcopal synodality without exercise of episcopal collegiality," Pope Francis's synodal vision, according to Massimo Faggioli, goes beyond "the idea of episcopal collegiality developed at Vatican II...Francis has made clear that the *theological* category of synodality includes, but at the same time also transcends the *juridical* principle of collegiality."[41] Applied to our understanding of justice and mercy, this means experiences gained from walking with the people of God informs the sharing and dialogue that takes place within and among the episcopate, wherein more awareness is created regarding the need for healing among the faithful. This vision appears to reconcile the possible tensions that may arise as we seek to understand the Petrine and Marian dimensions, and how they communicate the mercy and justice of God. Mercy, "God's perfect, compassionate, generous, kind and forgiving love, whether one feels worthy of it or not,"[42] offers healing, the therapeutic aspect of God's love, while justice, the habit of giving a person their due, whether it involves restoring balance through reward or offering correction or restitution, offers the juridical aspect of God's love, that is order and balance.[43]

An encounter with mercy can change someone for the better, especially if the person is humble. By contrast, as exemplified in the Parable of the Unforgiving Servant (Matthew 18:31–35), justice or correction is in order if an encounter with mercy does not produce fruit. If true repentance is not expressed, the person has not learned anything regarding the consequences of their behavior. The merciful mother, seeking to understand the intentions of the child, withholds correction if the child, moved and inspired by the mother's love, repents, and understands the implications of her actions. On the other hand, the just mother seeks to educate and correct when the child remains unchanged, lacking understanding. Recognizing and acknowledging what someone is feeling does not automatically result in the affirmation of those feelings, especially if the experience is not life-giving.

The correction, properly executed, is an extension of her healing love, seeking to restore order and help her child be better. To be clear, this is not about a male approach vs. a female approach, it is about learning how to relate to the people of God with God's love. The need for collaboration shows participants in the Petrine dimension how to be Marian and the way to proper accompaniment. Holding mercy and justice in balance prevents the people of God from exercising a legalistic approach to accompaniment, one that does not seek to understand the complexity of the human condition.[44] In my article on Pope Francis's Marian "program of life," I write:

> Just as the model of therapeutic jurisprudence reconciles the tension between mercy and justice, showing how love and truth are never in opposition, the Marian dimension of the Church complements and completes the Petrine dimension.[45]

Emphasis on the Marian dimension of the Church keeps the balance between the two actions of teaching and mothering or nurturing, to which all members of the Church are called. A parent who disciplines without nurture, risks causing harm.[46] Conversely, when a child knows she is loved unconditionally, the teaching is not going to rattle her, causing her to feel insecure and unloved. Instead, she will continue to approach her parent because there is no fear in the parenting style and if she doesn't understand, she will not be afraid to ask questions.

Marian Approaches to Synodality

What is key is to remain in a relationship with Mother Church as Jesus taught us to remain in a relationship with him (John 15:4). It is easier to receive and ponder Church teaching when the Church as Mother and Teacher emphasizes her love for her members. Listening, as one additional action, creates the foundation for effective teaching and formation, encouraging clergy and lay leaders to pay attention to the joys and sorrows of the people of God.

Julian of Norwich (b. 1343), a mystic inspired by private revelations regarding the mercy of God, received deep insights into the mercy-Mother/justice-Teacher dynamic. In the fourteenth of sixteen showings or private revelations, she came to understand the properties of motherhood revealed in Jesus, namely, mercy, grace, and nurture—how he feeds us with his body.[47] She describes how mercy and justice work together in divine parenting—the merciful mother loves the child unconditionally with tenderness. The just mother, without ceasing to love her child, disciplines when the child needs correction, which is necessary for the child to grow in virtue and grace.[48] Moreover, the "office of Motherhood"[49] she says, helps us to understand how Jesus loves and nurtures us:

> He does so most courteously and most tenderly, with the Blessed Sacrament, which is the precious food of true life. With all the sweet sacraments He sustains us most mercifully and graciously.[50]

This emphasis on Jesus's desire to nurture and protect is present in scripture. In his lament over Jerusalem, Jesus says, "How often have I desired to gather your children together as a hen gathers her brood under her wings" (Matt 23:37). If the Church, then, is the body of Christ, she must reveal to the world what it means to be Mother and Teacher. Mary, honoring the body of her son, is key to this process, including the process of divinization.

Mary

Divinization

Described by Julian as being "filled with grace and of all manner of virtues, passed beyond all other creatures,"[51] Mary demonstrates the offices of Mother and Teacher quite beautifully, showing how the Church is called to nurture and teach her children. Mary communicates how to be Church and how to be like God. Effectively, in Mary we see the fruit of divinization because *she is the first participant of the divine nature* (see 2 Pet 1:4). Divinization may be understood as cooperating with the transformative power of God's grace on the soul, making us more and more like God, perfecting the use of our free will and our intellect. Mary, according to Kevin Clarke, "plays an instrumental role in the restoration and the deification of humanity."[52]

Jesus, whose name means "God saves," became one of us so that we can be like him. Mary is like him; she is the sneak preview of humanity in a state of authentic freedom and spiritual harmony, integrated and receptive to the Holy Spirit. Jesus reveals a descending pattern, assuming our humanity, while Mary reveals an ascending pattern, showing us what it means to be divinized. A saying attributed to St. Fulgentius of Cartagena (d. 630) captures this mystery: "By Mary, God descended from Heaven into the world, so that by her we might ascend from Earth into Heaven." Similarly, in Mary, writes the mystic Adrienne von Speyr, "resides the idea of the perfect human being, an idea God had when he created the first human being."[53] This means that "the human being whom he, the Father, had in mind at the creation actually does exist."[54]

Mary, as Our Lady and the New Eve,[55] is the woman whom I call "the First Lady"—not in the more common sense of the title, meaning a wife of a head of state, but in the sense of a leader in her profession or state of life.[56] Mary is the First Lady of creation and of the Church. Consequently, the Petrine dimension can only flourish when it follows Mary's way of being and doing in the world. She, as "type and model of the Church," reveals the Church. This means living in communion with God reveals how to live in communion with others.

Commenting on this delicate tension, Pope Benedict XVI once said that the "Petrine aspect...is included in (the) Marian aspect. In Mary, the Immaculate, we find the essence of the Church without distortion." He went on to say, "In her, *God has impressed his own image*, the image of the One who follows the lost sheep even up to the mountains and among the briars and thorn bushes of the sins of this world."[57] This resembles the teaching found in the *Catechism of the Catholic Church*: "God's parental tenderness can also be expressed *by the image of motherhood*, which emphasizes God's immanence, the intimacy between Creator and creature" (239; emphasis mine).

Similarly, in his post-synodal apostolic exhortation on the Amazon, *Querida Amazonia*, Pope Francis affirmed the power of women to make God's love known in families and communities: "The Lord chose to reveal his power and his love through two human faces: the face of his divine Son made man and the face of a creature, a woman, Mary. Women make their contribution to the Church in a way that is properly theirs, by making present the tender strength of Mary, the Mother" (101). Mary reveals what it means to be Church, predisposing the hierarchy and lay leaders to the correct attitudes needed in order to do God's will. How does Mary know how to do God's will? The simple answer is her intimacy with the Holy Spirit, an intimacy accessible to all people of good will (*GS* 22), an experience key to the synodal process.

Mary and the Holy Spirit: A *Pneuma*-typical Approach

A *Pneuma*-typical approach to Mariology emphasizes Mary's intimacy with the Holy Spirit.[58] Mary reveals the Church in its perfected state, the Body of Christ, because, as Pope Benedict XVI affirmed, "In her, God has impressed his own image."[59] The moment of the incarnation represents the "first outpouring of the Holy Spirit upon her," says Pope John Paul II, making Mary the "image or model" of the Church.[60] Moreover, it is the power of God's grace at the moment of Mary's conception that made it possible for Mary to reveal the image of God in its original state, before the Fall.[61] Hence, the pneumatological dimension has anthropological implications for the study of human behavior. Although the dogma of the Immaculate Conception (1854) declares Mary was "preserved immune from all stain of original sin,"[62] helped by God's grace, "Mary remained free of every personal sin her whole life long."[63] Moreover, as a creature, a human, she would have cooperated with God's grace with constant prayer and discipline, especially during times of deep anguish and struggle. It is for this reason she has been referred to as the "temple of the Holy Spirit,"[64] a model St. Paul used to describe the dignity of the body and new life in the Spirit—a life accessible to everyone.[65]

In Mary, a creature like us, we have a sneak preview of the fulfillment of certain capacities with which we have been endowed, being created in God's image and likeness.[66] Mary, according to the CDF, is "chosen to reveal to men and women the way of love. Only in this way, can the 'image of God,' the sacred likeness inscribed in every man and woman, emerge according to the specific grace received by each (cf. Gen 1:27)."[67] Sadly, however, some may not know what it means to be created in God's image. Some may hear this expression and feel confused, especially if they have not been well catechized. Some may be wondering; does it mean we look like God? Understanding this mystery is key to understanding Mary as model of the Church and the power of the Holy Spirit in her life and in the life of those who desire to grow in holiness. To be created in

Marian Approaches to Synodality

God's image means we participate in God's being, thereby possessing the following:[68]

- Dignity (body and soul)[69]
- Capacity for self-knowledge/self-awareness
- Capacity for self-possession or self-control/self-mastery (a cardinal virtue and a fruit of the Spirit)
- Capacity for self-determination (free will)
- Capacity/freedom to enter into a loving relationship with others
- Capacity/freedom to accept God's grace, responding in faith and love

Mary, as a creature, reveals the glory of the person created in God's image, possessing authentic freedom, using one's intellect and free will to honor God, and reasoning and loving according to God's will. Thankfully, our cooperation with God's grace and the desire to do God's will can help us experience this state of authentic freedom. Although we are created in God's image, we continue to need grace to be like God (*CCC* 2784). The good news is grace acting on our souls, the process of divinization, restores the likeness. Ultimately, Mary models this process, beginning with the act of listening to the promptings of the Holy Spirit. Moreover, whenever we encounter someone with great self-awareness and self-knowledge, great self-regulation, and the capacity to reason and love, maintaining and sustaining relationships according to God's will, we encounter someone who is more and more like God.[70] God's love and grace, especially and experienced in early family life, can assist with the development and refinement of these capacities.[71] Moreover, being like God helps us to listen and accompany our brothers and sisters.

Listening to the Holy Spirit, the power of God's love, is key to the act of walking together.[72] Moreover, intimacy with

Mary

the Holy Spirit inspires a deep interior life. To be clear, the Holy Spirit guides the process of synodality. The formula *sentire cum ecclesia* refers to the practice of feeling, thinking, sensing, and perceiving in harmony with the Church.[73] Furthermore, the invocation of the Trinity, intimacy with the Word of God, Reconciliation, and the nourishment of the Eucharist, as "specific elements of Christian life," give help to Christians so that they can fulfil their mission in the world.[74] As an accompanying witness on the synodal journey, Mary models intimacy with the Holy Spirit—an intimacy that is well documented in sacred scripture and early Christian writings.

St. Maximus the Confessor, one of the most influential theologians of the early Byzantine period, prepared the earliest completed biography of Mary, *The Life of the Virgin*, in the seventh century.[75] Handing on what is believed to be the living memory of Mary's activity in the early Church, St. Maximus the Confessor's *The Life of the Virgin* gives the reader an insight into the ministry of Mary, the mother of Jesus, before and after his ascension. Following his analysis of the text, translator Stephen J. Shoemaker makes the following observation:

> Perhaps the most remarkable "new" material from the *Life* appears in its surprisingly developed account of Mary's active involvement in her son's ministry and her subsequent leadership of the apostles and the early church following his Ascension. In both instances Mary's representation in a position of spiritual and ecclesiastical authority stands in marked contrast with the tendency to minimize such roles for women in late ancient and early medieval Christianity.[76]

After the ascension, St. Maximus refers to Mary, the holy *Theotokos*, as a "participant and a leader in every good thing."[77] He continues:

Marian Approaches to Synodality

But she was not only an inspiration and a teacher of endurance and ministry to the blessed apostles and the other believers, she was also a co-minister with the disciples of the Lord. She helped with the preaching, and she shared mentally in their struggles and torments and imprisonments. And she suffered with them as she previously had shared the Passion of her Lord and son through sufferings of the heart. So now also she comforted his worthy disciples with actions as much as she could. She strengthened them with words and presented as an example for them the Passion of her king and son. She reminded them of the rewards and crowns of the kingdom of Heaven and the unending blessedness and delight unto the ages of ages.[78]

And she was the model of goodness and the teacher of excellence in the place of her Lord and son....And she was a leader and a teacher to the holy apostles, and when anything was needed, they would tell her. And they received direction and counsel from her, to the extent that those who were near the environs of Jerusalem would return.[79]

The activities described in *The Life of the Virgin* are supported by early liturgical images studied by scholar, Ally Kateusz, who has examined early scenes of Mary, depicting her as having influence in the early Church.[80] These images match St. Maximus's account of Mary's life, revealing Mary fulfilled the following roles in the years following the ascension:

- Inspirational teacher of excellence
- Cominister
- Preacher
- Cosufferer

Mary

- Comforter
- Model of goodness
- Leader
- Counselor/advisor

These roles are supported by her contributing and cooperating role in salvation history, including her presence in the upper room with the apostles. The Acts of the Apostles, describing the events leading up to the descent of the Holy Spirit, includes the names of the apostles waiting in the upper room "devoting themselves to prayer, *together with certain women, including Mary the mother of Jesus*" (Acts 1:14; emphasis mine). This represents the second outpouring of the Holy Spirit upon Mary:

> Responding to the prayer of the Blessed Virgin and the community gathered in the Upper Room on the day of Pentecost, the Holy Spirit bestows the fullness of his gifts on the Blessed Virgin and those present, working a deep transformation in them for the sake of spreading the Good News. The Mother of Christ and his disciples are granted new strength and new apostolic energy for the Church's growth. In particular, the outpouring of the Spirit leads Mary to exercise her spiritual motherhood in an exceptional way, through her presence imbued with charity and her witness of faith.[81]

The North American Final Document for the Continental Stage of the Synod references this moment in sacred scripture, reminding the faithful to "imitate Mary, who was present at the first Pentecost and continually said yes to the invitation to contribute to the building of the kingdom of God."[82]

This means Mary and "certain women" received the anointing of the Holy Spirit together with the apostles. Liturgical images

Marian Approaches to Synodality

abound of Mary sitting with the apostles in the upper room with tongues of fire resting on their heads. Just as Jesus is at the center of scenes depicting the Last Supper, Mary is positioned at the center in images depicting Pentecost. This scriptural and liturgical detail, along with other scriptural texts and Marian dogmas, confirms Mary's intimacy with the Holy Spirit.[83] Although, there is a line of succession that originates with the twelve apostles—the bishops as their successors, St. Maximus the Confessor explains that Mary, inspired by the Holy Spirit, was not only " an inspiration and a teacher of endurance and ministry to the blessed apostles and other believers, she was a co-minister"[84] who formed her own successors, women who ministered to other women.[85] Just as the Lord held authority "over the twelve disciples and then the seventy, *so did the holy mother over the other women who accompanied him.*"[86] Apart from the twelve apostles, whose successors went on to form the hierarchy of our Church, hence the expression apostolic succession, there was another category of apostles who were called by God to share the good news.

To be clear, what is being suggested here is not a parallel line of succession. Pope John Paul II, in his encyclical *Redemptoris Mater*, referring to Mary's presence in the Upper Room, writes, "*Mary did not directly receive this apostolic mission*" (*RM* 26). Although St. Maximus the Confessor goes deeper with his description of Mary's early activity, Pope John Paul II focuses on her unique witness and prayerful presence in the Upper Room (*RM* 26). Nevertheless, Mary participates in the Church's "apostolic witness" because she models the faith "that is passed on simultaneously through both the mind and the heart" (*RM* 28). A person cannot be sent to share the faith unless, like Mary, they have deepened their faith with God's grace and prayer.

An apostle, from the Greek *apostolos*, is one who is sent with a message. Even though St. Paul did not belong to the original twelve apostles, he refers to himself as an apostle.[87] Mary, and other early female disciples, on the other hand, were also sent with their own unique anointed mission. Apart from the twelve, St. Paul, Barnabas, and other men, some women have been referred to as apostles.[88] Although Paul's mission has been associated with the laying on of hands,[89] common to both categories of apostle, however, is the power of the Holy Spirit. We will develop this thought as we approach the final chapter.

Nevertheless, there is a striking resemblance between the words used to describe the power and action of the Holy Spirit and the words used to describe Mary's actions in the *Life of the Virgin* and in sacred scripture. New Testament scholar Joseph Chandrakanthan explains that the Greek word *parákletos* first appears in John 14:15: "And I will ask the Father, and he will give you another Advocate (*parákletos*), (helper) to be with you forever."[90] *Para* can be translated as "alongside or beside," and *kalein* can be translated as "to call." *Parákletos*, explains Dr. Chandrakanthan, can mean the following:

- Helper
- Teacher
- Guide
- Companion
- Friend
- Comforter
- Counselor
- Advocate/Intercessor

Take note of the similarity between the list of actions associated with the *parákletos* and the activities associated with the Blessed Virgin Mary in *The Life of the Virgin*, sacred scripture, and the teaching found in the Dogmatic Constitution on the Church, *Lumen Gentium*: "The Blessed Virgin is invoked by the Church under the titles of Advocate, *Auxiliatrix, Adjutrix*, and *Mediatrix*" (62). Notice the similarity between these titles and titles associated with the Holy Spirit such as advocate. *Auxiliatrix* is Latin for helper. The Greek equivalent is *parákletos*. Both *auxiliatrix* and *adjutrix* can be translated as helper, assistant, and aid. Moreover, the title *mediatrix* refers to Mary's maternal mediation, how her divine motherhood made possible by the action of the Holy Spirit at the moment of the incarnation makes her a powerful intercessor.[91]

Although magisterial teaching is clear regarding Mary's mediation being subordinate to Jesus's unique mediation (*LG* 62, *RM* 38), "her own mediation is a **shared mediation**" (*RM* 38) that has a "maternal character" because it is "intimately linked to her motherhood" (*RM* 38). The Holy Spirit makes her a "mother to us in the order of grace" (*RM* 38). Moreover, she gives a "total gift of self" (*RM* 39) in the "saving plans of the Most High" (*RM* 39). This is possible due to her intimacy with the Holy Spirit.

Perhaps it is for this reason—the overlapping activities performed by the Holy Spirit and our Blessed Mother—that St. Maximilian Kolbe was inspired to write: "The Third Person of the Blessed Trinity never took flesh; still our human word 'spouse' is far too weak to express the reality of the relationship between the *Immaculata* and the Holy Spirit. We can affirm that she is, in a certain sense, the 'incarnation' of the Holy Spirit."[92] According to St. Maximilian Kolbe, Mary, as the spouse of the Holy Spirit, is a *quasi incarnatus*.[93] In Latin, *quasi* means having some features but not all, or having some resemblance.

Moreover, Mary's connection to the power of the Holy Spirit is confirmed by the power of God's grace acting on her own soul when she was conceived in her mother's womb, the incarnation of Jesus, brought about by the power of the Holy Spirit, and the presence of the fruits of the Holy Spirit within her, visible to all whom encountered her. We rejoice that the same Spirit descended on the apostles, Mary, and "certain women," inspiring them to evangelize with courage and zeal.

Mary's presence and activity tick every box associated with the synodal journey, including the pneumatological and eucharistic connection.[94]

Her participation in the divine life provides the template for our own participation in God's being, showing us how to grow in holiness by using our gifts to evangelize and to inspire others to do the same. The next chapter will explore this insight further. Nevertheless, the power of the Holy Spirit allowed Mary to participate in an intimate way in the life of her son.

Mary and Her Son, Jesus: A *Christo*-typical Approach

A *Christo*-typical approach to Mariology is a more Christ-centered approach, emphasizing Mary's divine motherhood— Mary as the Mother of God, and her participation in the life of her son. Reflecting on Mary's connection to her son's ministry and suffering, which we will explore in greater detail later in this study, helps us to understand the profound intimacy they share and has implications for our understanding of Mary and the Eucharist. Mary's connection with Christ's body is twofold. First, during her pregnancy, she carries his body within hers, allowing the mystery of his divine being assuming her flesh, thereby creating an intimate bond between his experience of humanity and hers.[95] Second, Mary's experience of the crucifixion which creates another intense level of connection between his suffering and hers.

Regarding the first connection, we have already established Mary as type or model of the Church, precisely because she is the first partaker of the divine nature. With the help of the Holy Spirit, she gives birth to and reveals Christ's body to the world. Moreover, she embodies the fulfillment of the capacities with which we have been endowed, created in the image and likeness of God. Without doubt, God's grace strengthened Mary with these capacities so that she could endure the pain and suffering experienced with her son.[96]

On the topic of Mary's suffering, Pope John Paul II believed Mary's self-emptying at the foot of the cross was the deepest gift of self in human history.[97] As a model of the Church and synodality—walking and standing together, Mary stands with everyone who grieves the loss of a loved one, especially parents who have lost a child or witnessed the horrific death of a loved one. Mary's loss of her son, according to Maximus the Confessor, is a "second offering" to God.[98] Hence, there is a double offering—Mary offers her suffering to God and offers, with God, her son for our salvation. Thus, not only is Mary the first participant of the divine nature, but Mary is also *the first sharer in the sufferings of Christ*,[99] offering herself in the same way, as we, members of a royal priesthood, are called to offer up our own sufferings when we gather for the celebration of the Eucharist.[100] It is in this way that Mary, as an associate, participates in the sacrifice of Jesus, his priesthood. By uniting her sufferings to the sufferings of Jesus, "Mary inaugurates the Church's participation in the sacrifice of the Redeemer."[101]

Mary and the One Priesthood of Jesus Christ

Mary, *as the first participant in the one priesthood of Christ*, models a life of holiness for two expressions of this one priesthood: the ministerial priesthood (bishops and priests) and the common, royal, or baptismal priesthood, the baptized faithful, including permanent and transitional deacons.[102] Participation in the priesthood of Jesus reveals our mission as members of his Body. Commenting on the teaching of the Second Vatican Council, on the one priesthood of Christ, Pope John Paul II notes the necessity of the ministerial priesthood (bishops and priests) but also affirms how the baptized, including transitional

Mary

and permanent deacons, participate in the three-fold office of Christ—prophet, priest, and king—as members of the baptismal or common priesthood:

> The Second Vatican Council renewed the Church's awareness of the universality of the priesthood. In the New Covenant there is only one sacrifice and only one priest: Christ. *All the baptized share in the one priesthood of Christ*, both men and women, inasmuch as they must "present their bodies as a living sacrifice, holy and acceptable to God (cf. *Rom* 12:1), give witness to Christ in every place, and give an explanation to anyone who asks the reason for the hope in eternal life that is in them (cf. *1 Pet* 3:15)." Universal participation in Christ's sacrifice, in which the Redeemer has offered to the Father the whole world and humanity in particular, brings it about that all in the Church are "a kingdom of priests" *(Rev* 5:10; cf. 1 Pet 2:9), who not only share in the **priestly mission** but also in the **prophetic and kingly mission** of Christ the Messiah. Furthermore, this participation determines the organic unity of the Church, the People of God, with Christ. It expresses at the same time the "great mystery" described in the Letter to the Ephesians: *the bride united to her Bridegroom;* united, because she lives his life; united, because she shares in his threefold mission *(tria munera Christi);* united *in such a manner as to respond* with a "sincere gift" of self *to the inexpressible gift of the love of the Bridegroom,* the Redeemer of the world. This concerns everyone in the Church, women as well as men. It obviously concerns those who share in the ministerial priesthood," which is characterized by service. In the context of the "great mystery" of Christ and of

Marian Approaches to Synodality

the Church, all are called to respond—as a bride—with the gift of their lives to the inexpressible gift of the love of Christ, who alone, as the Redeemer of the world, is the Church's Bridegroom. The "royal priesthood," which is universal, at the same time expresses the gift of the Bride.[103]

To be Marian is to be an instrument of God's love, loving our neighbor with a sacrificial love, as members of the "royal priesthood" of Christ. To be Marian is to love, implying an intimacy with our God who is love (1 John 4:7–21). It is this sacrificial love that connects Mary, who models the way of love, to the sacrifice of her son, inspiring the controversial title "Virgin Priest."

The tradition of addressing Mary as "Virgin Priest" has been explored by medieval[104] and modern scholars, namely, René Laurentin.[105] Although scripture and magisterial teaching are clear regarding the *one* mediator, Jesus Christ,[106] Mary's *fiat* and presence at the foot of the cross demonstrate her own participation in the redeeming work of Jesus (*LG* 60–65). Mary's participatory mediation, however, is **secondary** to that of her son's (*LG* 60). Nonetheless, the image of Mary as Virgin Priest, used to express Mary's participation in Jesus's sacrifice, offering him to God, has been depicted in sacred art, leaving some confused, and some inspired, including various popes.

Between the seventh and ninth centuries, there is evidence of certain hymns including priestly titles for Mary.[107] Moreover, during the reign of Pius X, who served as pope between 1903 and 1914, there was a concern that Catholics would interpret the image and title of "Virgin Priest" to mean Mary received the sacrament of holy orders, implying the existence of a Marian priesthood. The Holy Office, formerly the CDF, now the Dicastery for the Doctrine of the Faith, responded to this dilemma by issuing a decree stating that "the representation of Mary clothed in sacerdotal vestments was disapproved."[108] Although the images were disapproved, it appears Pius X allowed prayers addressed to Mary as Virgin Priest.

Pius X approved a prayer based on Epiphanius's expression *sacerdos pariter et altare*, which concludes with the invocation *Maria Virgo sacerdos, ora pro nobis*. The prayer had been requested by the Daughters of the Sacred Heart of Jesus. The pope specified that although Mary had not received the sacrament of priestly ordination, she was endowed with its grace and dignity.[109]

Before this development, other popes were in favor of affirming Mary's participation in the sacrifice of Jesus, namely, Pope Pius IX, acknowledging her dignity and grace as "an associate of the Divine Sacrifice."[110] Being Jesus's mother creates for Mary a unique connection to the suffering of her son. It is in this way that she is an "associate," participating in his suffering. As an associate or helper, Mary is presented as a model for priestly ministry. This is the focus of René Laurentin's study of Mary, *Virgin Priest, Maria. Ecclesia, Sacerdotium: Essai sur le développement d'une idée religieuse,* linking Mary with priesthood "as a model for priestly purity."[111] This seems to support the idea that the Marian dimension precedes the Petrine dimension, meaning the priest must be like Mary before he can be another Christ—*in persona Christi capitis*. This implies the need for intimacy with Mary, affirming her love for all disciples, and her sharing in their sufferings as she shared in her son's. Mary models the "perfect love" of 1 John 4:18.

Similarly, Maximus the Confessor says the following regarding Mary's suffering and sacrifice, including her support of the grieving disciples:

> And she suffered with them as she had previously suffered the Passion of her Lord and Son through the sufferings of the heart. She now also comforted his

worthy disciples with actions as much as she could. She strengthened them with words and presented as an example for them the Passion of her king and Son. She reminded them of the rewards and crowns of the kingdom of heaven and the unending blessedness and delight unto the ages of ages.[112]

What is evidenced and honored here is Mary's work as a helpmate, an "associate," offering herself as a sacrifice, obedient to God's will, and together with God, offering her son for our salvation. This intimate partnership has inspired some to contemplate the mystery surrounding the connection between the Eucharist and Mary's and Jesus's suffering.

Mary and the Eucharist

According to John Paul II, the act of Mary offering her son is present at every Mass with us. He was convinced that "there is a fundamental link between Mary and the Eucharist."[113] Elsewhere he said, "This saving mystery in which God has assigned to the woman Mary of Nazareth, a role that cannot be replaced, is continually made present in the Eucharist. When we celebrate the Holy Mass, the Mother of the Son of God *is in our midst* and introduces us to the mystery of his redemptive sacrifice."[114]

According to Monsignor Arthur Burton Calkins, John Paul II, in his memorable Angelus address of Corpus Christi in June of 1983, broke new ground, highlighting the "profound link" between Mary's presence and the Eucharist. The words of John Paul II are striking: "Every mass puts us in intimate communion with her, the Mother, whose sacrifice 'becomes present' just as the sacrifice of her Son 'becomes present' at the words of the consecration of the bread and wine pronounced by the priest."[115]

This image is captured in a recent video production, "The Veil Removed" produced by Brenden Stanley.[116] The video shows the coming together of heaven and earth, designed to help the faithful imagine what is unseen during every Mass. Having watched the seven-minute or so video, I was delighted to see that Mary was included in the scene depicting the sacrifice of the Mass, showing Jesus crucified present, the heavenly host of angels, and Mary standing by the altar, at the foot of the cross. The scene recreates John's account of Jesus's crucifixion, with Mary standing in support for her son.[117]

Although Monsignor Calkins attributes this new theological development to John Paul II, René Laurentin, a priest and theologian who devoted the better part of his life to the study of Mary, recalls the autobiographical *Spiritual Journal* of St. Ignatius of Loyola, including the insight that "Ignatius saw Mary as an integral part of the Eucharist, to the point that he could perceive in an ineffable way how the flesh of Mary is present in the flesh of her Son (which she had given to him)."[118] St. Ignatius explains the moment he received this insight:

> While preparing at the altar, and after vesting, and during the Mass, very intense interior movements, and many intense tears and sobbing, with frequent loss of speech, and also after the end of Mass, and for long periods during the Mass, preparing and afterwards, the clear view of our Lady, very propitious before the Father, to such an extent, that in the prayers to the Father, to the Son, and at the consecration, I could not help feeling and seeing her, as though she were a part, or the doorway, of all the grace I felt in my soul. *At the consecration she showed that her flesh was in that of her Son*, with such great light that I cannot write about it."[119]

Although Jesus's and Mary's shared humanity must have inspired this insight, Ignatius, says Laurentin, does not "explain this inexpressible intuition further."[120] One thing that comes to mind, however, is how the Church is the Body of Christ and Mary is the model of the Church, showing us how to be the Body of Christ. This can only be possible because he takes his flesh from his mother; a mystical and physical union unites them. Nevertheless, Mary's presence, writes Monsignor Culkins, "serves as a guide for the Church in meditating on the mystery celebrated and in participating in the saving event and serves as the Church's model for generously participating in this sacrifice and, in a particular way, for offering to the Father the sacrifice of Christ and joining to it the offering of their own lives."[121] In other words, Mary models how being Church involves sacrificial love and experiencing Jesus in the Eucharist. Just as she joins God in offering up her son, we as members of the royal priesthood, are called to offer our own suffering, like her. Moreover, it shows how Mary and Jesus are united in one flesh, foreshadowing our communion with Jesus and one another when we receive the Eucharist. We are one body, and the Dogma of the Assumption of Mary reminds us of this mystery:

> Because her humanity stands closest to the humanity of Jesus, which has passed through death to a new, indestructible life suffused with his own divinity, because she is still "one body" with Jesus, Mary is the first to experience the full transformation of body and spirit—the "divinization" of what is human—that is promised to everyone who becomes "one body" with him in faith and baptism.[122]

The reflection on Mary's experience of divinization and her presence during the sacrifice of the Mass affirms Mary's presence in the Church, showing how she can be known through a thoughtful study of scripture, liturgy, archeology, iconography, devotions, theological discourse, and most especially

Mary

through invocation.[123] Her presence, however, is not limited to these means. The synodal process depends on this relationship, including a more insightful study of what it means to be Marian and how to make her presence known throughout the process. Although John Paul II described Mary's presence as "active and exemplary," "essential," "permanent," "maternal," and "special,"[124] more can be said about women making Mary's presence known.

René Laurentin, who like John Paul II, said similar things about Mary's presence, asks, "So what is there about Mary's presence that depends on us?"[125] I intend to offer a response to this question in the next chapter where I explore the role of women in the Church, showing how listening and the call to communion are deeply Marian. Making Mary's presence known throughout this process depends, not only on the Petrine dimension, but also on the presence of women. They, like Mary, are called to be accompanying witnesses throughout the synodal process. They, too, are called to be:

- Participants of the divine nature
- Participants/sharers in the suffering and glory of Christ
- Participants in the one priesthood of Christ

As we prepare to listen, understand, and act like Mary on the synodal path, may we remember how we are called to be like her, "the true face of the Church":

> The Church desires that Christian women should become more fully aware of the greatness of their mission; today their role is of capital importance, both for the renewal and humanization of society and for the rediscovery of believers of the *true face* of the Church.[126]

3

The Church Listening
A Marian Approach

In Mary, we find all the essential attitudes necessary for the synodal path, beginning with humility. Humility, according to the ITC, "inclines each one to be obedient to God's will and obedient to each other in Christ."[1] Other essentials attitudes listed in the *Vademecum*, or guidebook, include sharing, dialogue, openness, and discernment.[2] These attitudes are deeply Marian, meaning they exemplify what it means to be receptive to the promptings of the Holy Spirit.

In Luke's Gospel, in the account of the annunciation, marking the moment of the incarnation, we discover the encounter between the archangel Gabriel and Mary of Nazareth (1:26–38). Mary's listening and responding to the words of Gabriel can be framed as a dialogue in three phases: pondering the perplexity of the address (1:29),[3] questioning with sincerity the revelation (1:34), and finally acceptance or her *fiat* "Here am I, the servant of the Lord; let it be with me according to your word" (1:38). Mary manages her perplexity with deep pondering, meaning she approached this announcement with careful thought, not limiting her response to an impulsive rejection of what could

The Church Listening

have been considered a startling impossibility. Instead, her pondering leads to heroic trust and obedience to God's will. In effect, she models discernment and what it means to be fully present to God, culminating in the experience of the fruits of the Spirit.

The temptation, however, is to forget she was perplexed and needed to ponder the greeting and the message, including the need to ask a question. Her questioning, however, was not due to malice or the desire to test the angel, rather Mary was sincere in her desire to understand this key moment in salvation history.[4] Cardinal Joseph Ratzinger writes, "In other words, Mary enters an interior dialogue with the Word. She carries on an inner dialogue with the Word that has been given her; she speaks to it and lets it speak to her, in order to grasp its meaning."[5] Her question focused on **how** the conception of Jesus will take place because she is a virgin (Luke 1:34). The archangel Gabriel reassures her, "The Holy Spirit will come upon you, and the power of the Most High will overshadow you; therefore the child to be born will be holy; he will be called Son of God" (Luke 1:35). Accompanied by the power of the Holy Spirit, Mary is open to this process because she is "full of grace."[6]

God's gift of grace—the free, unmerited gift of supernatural strengthening and power—is within Mary. Not only is she full of this power, but she is also assured that she is not alone because the Lord is with her (Luke 1:28). Dr. Edward Sri, author of *Walking with Mary*, explains that "'The Lord is with you' signals that someone is being called to a great mission that will be difficult and demanding."[7] Mary has courage to ask questions and to respond to God's will with complete surrender because, knowing she is loved, she is strengthened by God's grace. Reassured that the "power of the Most High" (Luke 1:35) will envelope her, accompanying her throughout her life, Mary's faith becomes bigger than her fear. This affirmation gives her the courage to trust God's plan, knowing her *fiat* was possible due to grace, accompaniment, and surrender. Let us consider

Mary's approach to listening and responding as we examine the synodal input on the role of women in the Church, acknowledging the need for God's grace and careful thought before we can understand the role of women with greater clarity.

The synodal act of listening allows for questions and dialogue, especially where there is perplexity; however, authentic listening requires humility and intimacy with the Holy Spirit—communion. As we have seen in the previous chapter, following Mary's way of listening requires this level of intimacy, obedience, trust, and most especially closeness to the sacraments. Among other outcomes, the fruit of following the Holy Spirit includes joy, peace, and patience (Gal 5:22–23). Accordingly, checking for the fruits of the Spirit is part of the discernment process. Unity, another sign of intimacy with the Holy Spirit, can only come about after a time of humble reflection, discernment, and attentive listening to the promptings of the Holy Spirit. Moreover, if there is fear in our discernment on this issue, we risk experiencing confusion and division. Nevertheless, as we continue our conversation, let us consider some of the responses to the synodal questionnaire.

Synodal Input

At the time of this writing, the Continental Phase of the synodal process had ended with the release of continental reports. Previously, the Diocesan Phase culminated in the drafting of diocesan syntheses forwarded to their episcopal conferences. Using this input, episcopal conferences and synods of Oriental Churches prepared national syntheses based on the reports gathered in the diocesan phase. The synthesis of these national reports informed the writing of *"Enlarge the Space of Your Tent" (Isa 54:2): Working Document for the Continental Stage (DCS).*[8]

The National Synthesis for Canada (2022) was submitted in September of 2022.[9] The national report "retained what was most present in the four reports" of the four Regional Assemblies.[10] Among other issues, the reports emphasized the need for reconciliation with indigenous peoples,[11] calling on "Church leaders to take more decisive action with indigenous peoples to assist in the healing of those wounded by the Church, particularly by the Indian Residential School system and its legacy."[12] Earlier in the year, Pope Francis's visit to Canada, the theme of which was "Walking Together," signaled the need to genuinely listen and walk in greater humility.[13]

Another key issue that surfaced in the various reports involved a discussion around greater collaboration and coresponsibility among clergy and laypeople, men, and women. Additionally, better training for laity was emphasized.[14] Similar input is found in the *National Synthesis of the People of God in the United States of America*.[15]

The American synthesis, like the Canadian one, addressed the many comments made on the topic of "enduring wounds." "Chief among the enduring wounds that afflict the People of God in the United States is the unfolding effects of the sexual abuse crisis."[16] Comments noted the erosion of trust in the hierarchy of the Church and the loss of credibility. This wound, together with ideological divisions, have led to greater polarization and marginalization.[17] Among the groups identified as experiencing marginalization, women indicated they felt marginalized "in the decision-making process of the Church, especially women of parish staff feeling underappreciated, underpaid, not supported in seeking formation, worked long hours, and lacked good role models for self-care."[18]

Most of the American synodal consultations revealed a "deep appreciation" for the contribution of lay women, including consecrated persons, in their parish communities. People recommended the promotion of stronger leadership roles for women, including preaching and a more formal pathway for women in ministry. What should be noted, however, is only seven hundred thousand participants responded to the American synodal consultations, meaning a small percentage of the almost fifty-one million Catholics in the United States of America participated in the process.[19] Some critics have noted that the low rate of participation does not reflect the views of all Catholics.[20] Nevertheless, those who participated expressed their concerns and shared their observations with the Church.

Overall, both syntheses, the American and the Canadian, call for greater coresponsibility between clergy and the laity. Similarly, *"Enlarge the Space of Your Tent" (Isa 54:2): Working Document for the Continental Stage* includes a synthesis of the findings in this area. Interestingly, St. John of Damascus in a homily on the dormition of Mary wrote, "The tent of Abraham, too, quite obviously signified you (cf. Gen 18:6)."[21] Similarly, St. Maximus the Confessor, in a litany dedicated to Mary, refers to her as "the tent of the Word of God."[22] The North American Synod Team notes that Jesus, is "the centre of the tent,"[23] and Mary, as the tent, images the Church, embracing her children, providing shelter. Moreover, enlarging the tent implies welcoming the gifts of the people of God, signaling the call for greater participation. Of this, the *Document for the Continental Stage* noted that the "call for a conversion of the Church's culture, for the salvation of the world, is linked in concrete terms to the possibility of establishing a new culture, with new practices and structures. A critical and urgent area in this regard concerns the role of women and their vocation, rooted in our common baptismal dignity, to participate fully in the life of the Church."[24] Rethinking women's participation, the document notes, involves women being "valued first and foremost as baptized and equal members of the People of God."[25] Similarly, the *North American Final Document for the Continental Stage* called for greater discernment regarding the "faithful acknowledgment of women's baptismal dignity."[26] Although most reports raised the issue of greater participation of women, including the areas of governance and decision-making,[27] there continues to be tension regarding a clear role for women:

> The reports do not agree on *a single or complete* response to the question of the vocation, inclusion and flourishing of women in Church and society. After careful listening, many reports ask that the Church continue its discernment in relation to a range of specific questions: the active role of women in the governing structures of Church bodies, the possibility for women with adequate training to preach in parish settings, and a female diaconate.[28]

Evidently, those contributing their ideas to the synodal process are calling for more discernment on the role of women in the Church, including more leadership roles and pastoral training, especially because there is no agreement on a "single or complete" response. Without doubt, this is due to the diversity of women who submitted input, showing we are not all the same—a key observation made by others.[29] The experience of women varies across the globe, giving rise to different concerns and approaches to the role of women in the Church. While it is beyond the scope of this chapter to offer a complete response to this issue, following the lead of the preparatory documents, the various documents prepared during the Continental Stage, and the *Instrumentum laboris*, I intend to focus on the need to raise awareness regarding the fulfillment of the common mission of the baptismal or royal priesthood, including the rights and obligations of the laity, especially when it comes to women and ministry. In other words, I intend to address the question posed in the *IL* regarding the baptismal dignity of women: "How can the Church of our time better fulfill its mission through greater recognition and promotion of the baptismal dignity of women?"[30]

The *North American Final Document for the Continental Stage* urged that "we need to ground ourselves in the equal dignity of baptism. This is an entry point for co-responsibility."[31] Similarly, the Australian bishops, in their final document for the continental stage, indicated "greater formation for deeper understanding of this reality" is needed to "empower people."[32] Knowing who we are and what we can do provides the foundation for further study and developments regarding women and ministry.

Keeping the focus on Mary and the Marian dimension, I intend to emphasize greater collaboration between clergy and laity, including consecrated persons, thereby proposing new pathways for women anchored in the baptismal priesthood. To address these issues, let us return to the Marian framework introduced at the beginning of this chapter, using it to explore how the synodal process can facilitate the listening that is required when it comes to women and ministry. To listen, according to Susan Bigelow Reynolds, "is to emulate God's own fundamental disposition towards God's people."[33] Let us examine this question with fidelity and openness to the guidance of the Holy Spirit.

Pondering the Perplexity: Women in Ministry

> Yes, and I ask you also, my loyal companion, help these women, for they have struggled beside me in the work of the gospel, together with Clement and the rest of my co-workers, whose names are in the book of life. (Phil 4:3)

On November 22, 2022, in an exclusive interview with five representatives of *America* media, Pope Francis was asked a question about the role of women in the Church.[34] Alas,

The Church Listening

according to the responses, there continues to be confusion and perplexity surrounding the issue of women in ministry. Previous discussions and consultations throughout the years reveal the vocation of women to be "a subject of constant human and Christian reflection,"[35] surfacing yet again during the global synodal consultations. As the Church continues to walk with women, dialogue regarding this issue is key to deepening our understanding.

Pope Francis, in calling for the Synod on Synodality and consenting to participate in this interview, demonstrates that he is open to dialogue. In his response to the question on women in the Church, he echoes our discussion in chapter 2 on the necessity of the Marian principle or dimension of the Church, calling for greater emphasis on understanding the Church as "mother and spouse,"[36] encouraging catechesis in the Marian principle, creating greater awareness, and developing our understanding of what it means for women to participate in the Marian principle. Naming an additional ecclesial principle, he explained there are three principles guiding the movement of the Church, "two theological and one administrative," namely,

> the Petrine principle, which is the ministerial dimension, but the church cannot function only with that one. The Marian principle, which is that of the spousal church, the church as spouse, the church as woman. And the administrative principle, which is not theological, but is rather that of administration, about what one does.[37]

Before we continue with more analysis, it might be helpful to review why Pope Francis is referring to the spousal meaning of the Church. St. Paul's Letter to the Ephesians builds on Jesus's self-understanding as bridegroom[38] and refers to the Church as the bride, his body.[39] Referring back to the teaching in Genesis

Marian Approaches to Synodality

regarding man and woman becoming one flesh, St. Paul uses this analogy to explain the desired unity between the members of the body and Christ as our head. Moreover, official Church teaching recognizes Jesus's death on the cross as the moment the Church is born, the origin of the Church, coming forth from the water and blood gushing from the side of his body in the same way Eve comes forth from Adam's side, his rib: "As Eve was formed from the sleeping Adam's side, so the Church was born from the pierced heart of Christ hanging dead on the cross" (*CCC* 766). The model of the Church as Bride of Christ applies to all the faithful, male and female. Nevertheless, Pope Francis emphasizes the Marian influence present in the Church as "woman," described by the CDF as a "mystical identity, profound and essential."[40]

Like Eve, the Church is Jesus's helpmate or associate, or as we have seen, the role exemplified by Mary, the New Eve. As he has done before,[41] of the three dimensions, Pope Francis goes on to declare the Marian principle to be the most important. Although, he says, the Petrine principle "has no place" for ordained ministry for women,[42] women can and do participate in the administrative principle; however, he says, the Marian principle is much more, meaning we cannot rely on the administrative principle to "explain it." This implies the Marian principle is more than leadership and decision-making.

To clarify his remarks, the pope went on to affirm the deep insight of women by showing how women must be involved in the discernment process with candidates for the priesthood, remarking how their intuition regarding certain candidates is to be trusted; therefore, he says, "the advice of a woman is very important, and the decision of a woman is better."[43] Moreover, at the end of his four-day visit to Bahrain in 2022, he said, "I have seen that in the Vatican, every time a woman comes in to do a job in the Vatican, things get better."[44] Pope Francis is showing how one cannot appreciate the gifts of women unless one experiences women in ministry and leadership. Overall, in affirming the Marian principle for women, he affirms Mary's role in our walk with God, walking in the Spirit, revealing our higher purpose for the greater good.

Pia de Solenni, in her response to Pope Francis's interview with *America* magazine, would like to see the conversation about the vocation of women "move beyond the topic of priestly vocation," encouraging the faithful to spend some time "unpacking the mystery she (Mary) holds for all of us" as she was "the first teacher of Jesus."[45] Similarly, Abigail Favale, responding to the same interview, comments that "the Marian principle which Francis highlights alongside the Petrine principle, does not have a clear institutional expression in the current structure of the church hierarchy. What would it look like to create one?"[46] Hopefully, this reflection on Mary and synodality will contribute to this discussion, showing how Mary reveals a pathway forward for women, thereby paving the way for a "clear institutional expression" or a unique vocation for women.

Hence, in responding to Pope Francis's call to deepen our understanding of the Church as Mother, the Marian dimension, the question becomes, how do we catechize regarding this calling? How do we raise awareness regarding the participation of women in the mission of the Church? What do women reveal regarding how to walk with people in this synodal journey? Or, as Reynolds asks, "What would it mean for women to be recognized as protagonists in the Church, as full subjects, diverse in every respect, with the agency to respond in freedom and creativity to the call of the Gospel?"[47] As initial steps, we can raise awareness regarding this calling by emphasizing the following in our catechetical efforts:

- The gift of our baptism
- Lay collaboration in ministry
- The gifts of women

Knowing who we are is the first step in the discernment process. Anchoring us in God's love that informs our identity, the Holy Spirit reveals our gifts and establishes our mission. Mary's identity was revealed as "favored one" and "full of grace" (Luke 1:28), preparing her to embrace her mission. We, too, benefit from knowing our baptismal identity before we embrace our mission.

Baptism

The *North American Final Document for the Continental Stage* reminds us we are called and gifted through baptism (14). Moreover, baptism "grounds our common identity and participation in Christ and the Church."[48] The *Catechism* states:

> Baptism is the basis of the whole Christian life, the gateway to life in the Spirit, and the door which gives access to the other sacraments. Through Baptism we are freed from sin and reborn as sons of God; we become members of Christ, are incorporated into the Church and made sharers in her mission. (1213)
>
> The anointing with sacred chrism signifies our anointing by the Holy Spirit, incorporating us into Christ who is "anointed priest, prophet, and king." (1241)

On the day of our baptism, we were sealed with "the indelible spiritual mark" or character of belonging to Christ (*CCC* 1272). We die and rise with Christ, becoming a "new creature" (1214). Moreover, Confirmation seals baptismal grace (1285), and we receive the Holy Spirit.

By becoming members of the baptismal priesthood, or the common priesthood of believers (1268, 1273), we are "partakers of the divine nature" (1265, cf. 2 Pet 1:4.), receiving sanctifying grace that makes it possible to live holy lives, to be charitable, to know and love God, and to experience intimacy with the Holy Spirit (1273, 1276). In other words, the sacrament of baptism confirms the following:

- We participate in the priesthood of Jesus.
- We are "partakers of the divine nature."
- We share in Christ's death and resurrection.
- We share in Christ's mission.

Compare our Church's teaching on the "common dignity deriving from our baptism"[49] with our previous discussion of Mary's participation in the Church. Walking like Mary involves living out our baptismal identity. Just as she reveals the Church in her perfected state, she reveals the fullness of our identity as God's adopted sons and daughters (see Rom 8:15). Interestingly, Pope John Paul II, during the Marian Year (1987–88), prepared *Mulieris Dignitatem*, an Apostolic Letter on the Dignity and Vocation of Women in which he gives Mary as an example of the fulfillment of the human person, showing us what it means to be human. In other words, he reminds us of our baptismal identity, showing us what it means to be like God.

In the catechesis on the deeper meaning of the sacrament of baptism, we discover two models of the Church used to describe the process of initiation, that of Church as Teacher and as Mother; formation joins us to Christ our teacher, and we are welcomed, embraced, and loved by Church as Mother (*CCC* 1248, 1249). As was discussed in chapter 2, Mary was the first participant of the divine nature, the first participant in the priesthood of Jesus, the first participant in the suffering of Jesus, and the first participant in the mission of Jesus. The sacrament of baptism, like the life of Mary, reveals our unique calling. She models how to be Church and how to walk and stand with the people of God.

The Marian principle represents receptivity to this process that begins with our baptism. If we haven't received anything, how can we be instruments of sharing God's love? Receptivity comes before productivity. The unfolding of this process, by extension, nurtures our vocation, reminding us to participate by using our gifts to feed the people of God. Pondering the deeper meaning of our baptism, with the help of good catechesis, should remove some of the perplexity surrounding our unique and shared mission in the life of the Church. Mission, then, begins with knowing our identity and purpose. Knowing who Mary is helps us to know who we are called to be. This helps us to consider the question of lay collaboration, knowing what we can do as members of the baptismal priesthood. This brings us to the second phase of the Marian framework for listening. Taking the time to learn and understand our Church's teaching on the apostolate of the lay faithful is the next step in our discernment. This task will help us to know with greater clarity God's plan for the use of our gifts.

Questioning: A Careful Consideration (What Can Women Do?)

One of the courses I teach at St. Augustine's Seminary in Scarborough, Ontario, Canada, is Lay Ministry in the Diocesan Church. One key area addressed throughout the course is lay collaboration with clergy, emphasizing the important mission of the laity. Apart from highlighting the teaching of the Second Vatican Council on the "universal call to holiness" (*LG* 39–42) for all states of life in the Church, we study the rights and obligations of the lay faithful.[50] In other words, the content of the course addresses other key questions raised in the *Instrumentum laboris*: "How can preaching, catechesis and pastoral work promote a shared awareness of the meaning and context of mission? How can it convey that mission constitutes a real and concrete call for every baptized person?"[51]

Students respond with amazement after they learn about the positive developments that have occurred, especially when comparing the mention of the laity in the 1917 Code of Canon Law and the rights and obligations of the laity documented in the 1983 Code, which reflects the development that accompanied the teaching of the Second Vatican Council.[52] The 1917 Code includes two canons on the laity: one declaring the right of laity to receive "from the clergy spiritual goods of the church" and a second prohibiting laity "from wearing clerical dress unless they were seminarians."[53]

By contrast, the new Code of 1983, in book 2 on "The People of God" includes twenty-four canons (cc. 208–31) that incorporate the teaching of the Second Vatican Council on the rights of the laity, affirming the baptismal priesthood of the laity, thereby showing how we are equal in dignity and how we share in Christ's priestly, prophetic, and royal functions.[54] One key right includes the right of parents to educate their children and to evangelize (c. 211). Using the Dogmatic Constitution on the Church, *Lumen Gentium* (1965) and the Decree on the Apostolate on the Laity, *Apostolicam Actuositatem* (1965), the 1983 Code of Canon Law articulated the developed teaching on the activity of the laity, documenting how laity may collaborate with clergy. Apart from receiving proper formation and training, to cominister in parishes, study, and teach theology (*AA* 28–32), other capacities include but are not limited to:

- Holding ecclesiastical offices (cc. 145, 228 §1)
- Assisting with governance (c. 129)
- Serving as chancellor of a diocese (c. 483)
- Holding a position within a marriage tribunal (cc. 1421, 1428, 1435)
- Serving on diocesan councils (cc. 492-94, 537)

Marian Approaches to Synodality

- Caring for a parish in the absence of a priest (c. 517, §2)
- Preaching (c. 766)

Moreover, as their main mission, laity are called to *renew the temporal order*[55] and to organize themselves as members of groups or lay associations (*AA* 15). Encouraged to share their gifts in their local communities and beyond, magisterial teaching affirms lay leadership and influence in a variety of sectors, including many Vatican offices.[56] Recently, Pope Francis, in his Apostolic Constitution, *Preadicate Evangelium*, declared that members of the faithful can lead one of the newly constituted Vatican dicasteries.[57] This is a significant development, building on the teaching of his predecessors.

Pope John Paul II, in his 1988 post-synodal apostolic exhortation on the laity, "On the Vocation and the Mission of the Lay Faithful in the Church and in the World," *Christifideles Laici*, uses the image of a vine to capture the work of the lay faithful. Rooted in the life of the Trinity, baptized persons branch out into various sectors, using their gifts and sharing their love with others. He writes, "Every area of the lay faithful's lives, as different as they are, enters into the plan of God, who desires that these very areas be the 'places in time' where the love of Christ is revealed and realized for both the glory of the Father and the service of others."[58] Clearly, the vocation of the laity has been affirmed, reminding them of their unique contributions. Among those laity have been countless women who have sustained the Church throughout the world.

Women, including consecrated women, have continued to minister to the people of God throughout the centuries. Indeed, Pope Francis credits women with keeping the Church alive in the Amazon: "In the Amazon, there are communities that have long preserved and handed on the faith even though no priest has come their way, even for decades. This could happen

The Church Listening

because of the presence of strong and generous women who, undoubtedly called and prompted by the Holy Spirit, baptized, and catechized, prayed, and acted as missionaries."[59]

These women are textbook examples of the interdicasterial 1997 "Instruction on Certain Questions Regarding the Collaboration of the Non-ordained Faithful in the Sacred Ministry of Priest," prepared by eight Vatican departments.[60] The document provides instruction regarding ministry in places and times when clergy are not available. While the document authors affirm the relationship between the ministerial priesthood and the common priesthood, how they are "ordered one to another," as an extension of the one priesthood of Christ, they call for an awakening and deepening "co-responsibility."[61] Although they are "two ways complementary ways of sharing in the one Priesthood of Christ...these two ways...are different 'essentially and not only in degree.'"[62]

The common priesthood originates in the sacrament of baptism, whereas, the ministerial priesthood, bishops, and priests (*CCC* 1554), is founded through the sacrament of holy orders, conferring special powers and duties. Notwithstanding the distinction between the ministerial priesthood and the baptismal or common priesthood, it is interesting to note that the ministries available to trained and specially selected laypeople, especially in times of emergency, signal greater coresponsibility, including ministries usually carried out by permanent deacons, namely,

- Sunday Celebrations in the Absence of a Priest (Article 7)
- Assistance at Marriages (Article 10)
- The Minister of Baptism (Article 11)[63]
- Leading the Celebration at Funerals (Article 12)

Moreover, canon law instructs that a layperson could be appointed to care for a parish if there are an insufficient number of priests (c. 512, §2). It seems as though this instruction would allow for bishops to prepare for a time of struggle, by appointing a few, let's say, "first responders" in their diocese in the event of a disaster or national emergency. These trained "first responders" could be called upon to assist in a crisis. Women could be trained to be these "first responders," as in the case of the Amazon. Although the object of the instruction on collaboration "is to outline specific directives to ensure the effective collaboration of the non-ordained faithful in such circumstances while safeguarding the integrity of the pastoral ministry of priests,"[64] it does affirm the need for greater coresponsibility, acknowledging the charisms and baptismal identity of the laity, including catechesis and evangelization of which preaching is a part.

Lay preaching is permitted and encouraged in certain contexts;[65] however, canon law makes it clear that lay preaching is not to occur within the celebration of the Mass in the space reserved for the homily.[66] As long as there is no confusion with the homily, it is permitted that laypeople can preach, facilitate conferences, and offer instruction in other pastoral contexts, such as retreats, prayer services, and parish missions outside of Mass. Diocesan bishops may allow lay faithful to preach when they judge it to be "to the spiritual advantage of the faithful," as long as the lay preacher is "orthodox in faith, and well-qualified, both by the witness of their lives as Christians and by a preparation for preaching appropriate to the circumstances."[67]

While there are restrictions placed on lay preaching, the Directory of Masses for Children, published by the Congregation for Divine Worship in 1973, states that "one of the adults may speak after the gospel, especially if the priest finds it hard to adapt himself to the mentality of children" (24). Indeed, this means there are opportunities for qualified, faith-filled laypeople to preach, including formation for women preachers.[68]

Following in the footsteps of some early female evangelists, these women, called by Jesus, have Mary as their model, who according to Maximus the Confessor "helped with the preaching," sharing mentally "in the struggles, and torments, and imprisonments" of the apostles and early disciples.[69] Evidently, Mary and other female preachers received the anointing to preach from the Holy Spirit.[70]

Because the female is created in God's image, her experience allows her to bring a certain insight into the human condition, sharing her wisdom with others. Moreover, the Holy Spirit has inspired women to be instruments of God's love and truth, including St. Mary Magdalene, "the apostle to the apostles,"[71] present in all four Gospel accounts of the empty tomb, as the first witness sent to share the good news of the resurrection with the apostles.

In Matthew's account of the empty tomb, the angel of the Lord says to Mary Magdalene and the other Mary to "go quickly and tell his (Jesus's) disciples, 'He has been raised from the dead,'" (Matt 28:7). Later Jesus meets them and says, "Do not be afraid; go and tell my brothers to go to Galilee; there they will see me" (Matt 28:10). The remaining three Gospel accounts include similar details regarding the women and the empty tomb.[72] Jesus could have appeared first to the male apostles, instead he chose to appear to the women because according to Pope Francis "they were the first to go to the tomb" and were "not paralyzed by sadness and fear."[73]

Their witness to the resurrection is a striking detail, as a Jewish court of law did not consider the testimony of women to be legally valid.[74] To honor this special encounter with Jesus, Pope Francis, in 2016, raised the rank of the memorial of St. Mary Magdalene, July 22, to a feast in the liturgical calendar. "This means that not only will the special readings for the day be proclaimed, but the Gloria will be prayed, and, for the first time ever, a special Preface to the Eucharistic Prayer will be included in the celebration of the Mass. The Preface is titled "Apostle to the Apostles," the honorific bestowed upon Mary Magdalene."[75]

Marian Approaches to Synodality

Similarly, St. Photine, or the Samaritan woman at the well, considered "equal to the apostles," was sent to share her encounter with the Messiah with fellow Samaritans (John 4:1–54. Just as Philip says "come and see" to Nathaniel (John 1:46), St. Photine says "come and see" to her fellow Samaritans (John 4: 29). Another woman sent on a mission, St. Hildegard of Bingen, Doctor of the Church and a travelling preacher and scientist, considered herself the "trumpet of God."[76] Likewise, St. Catherine of Siena, a laywoman and third-order Dominican, also a preacher and a Doctor of the Church, was celebrated by Pope Paul VI for her charism of "wisdom in discourse."[77] These women, among many others, are evangelists, proposing and re-proposing the good news to God's people in retreats, conferences, and prayer services.

Exposure to female preaching helps people gain insight into female experience and knowledge of the divine, both sources for theological discussion. Women, of all states of life, share a unique perspective and will give the people of God a women's view into the plight of families, the joys and challenges of marriage and parenting, experiences of consecrated life, and other experiences gained serving in a variety of sectors.[78] Furthermore, they give a unique perspective into the life of Mary, seeing themselves in her experiences. All these activities bear witness to the fruit that comes with collaboration and coresponsibility between the ministerial priesthood and the royal priesthood of the baptized. The desire for greater collaboration provides more opportunities for women in ministry, especially exposing the people of God to their gifts, and hopefully, removing some of the fear around seeing more women in leadership roles. Although Pope Francis, in continuity with his predecessors, resists the call to clericalize women, he encourages women to make "present the tender strength of Mary."[79]

Having reviewed some of the ministerial activity of the laity, there is ample opportunity for laypeople to use and share their gifts, albeit some in a limited context such as an emergency, and only after approval and formal training.[80] Although it is the role of the laity to renew "the temporal order" (*AA* 7) by evangelizing in the various sectors where they live and work, their gifts are needed to promote the flourishing of a variety of ministries. Laypeople participate in these ministries by virtue of their baptism, as members of the baptismal priesthood. Nonetheless, the challenge becomes creating awareness among clergy and laity regarding the rights and obligations of the laity. Hence, widespread catechesis is necessary, providing a foundation for dialogue concerning women and ministry.

We have unpacked the deeper meaning of the Marian principle in relation to our baptismal priesthood. We have pondered the Church's teaching regarding what laity, especially what women can do. Let us move into the next phase of the Marian framework for listening and seeking to know and discern God's will as the Church walks with women, including the example of some lay apostolates and the fruits of this activity.

Discerning God's Will

Following a Marian approach to synodality, pondering with humility, questioning with careful consideration and sincerity, submitting to the promptings of the Holy Spirit, and leading us to know God's will, let us now consider the implications of this study, including the possibility of creating new pathways for women in ministry. The ITC in *Synodality in the Life of the Church* states that "an essential attitude in synodal dialogue is humility, which inclines each one to be obedient to God's will and obedient to each other in Christ" (112).

The questioning phase of the listening process included questions raised by Superiors General, previous synods, scholars, commissions, and the people of God as evidenced in the syntheses prepared by 112 out of 114 episcopal conferences[81] and a video prepared by synod.va,[82] including the input of fourteen women appointed to review the synodal process and the need for more women in decision-making roles. The discussion around women, they say, is authentic and will continue, listening to the needs of the people of God and looking for a way forward for women in more leadership roles. As we ponder these requests for clarity and deeper insight into the role of women, it is helpful to review some data pertaining to the activity of women in the Church.

Together, men and women have witnessed to Christ's love and truth in a variety of contexts, reaching back to the early days of Christianity. *The Decree on the Lay Apostolate* from the Second Vatican Council affirms these heroic acts of service: "Sacred Scripture shows how spontaneous and fruitful such activity was at the very beginning of the Church."[83] Similarly, Pope St. John Paul II referred to these witnesses as "co-laborers in the vineyard."[84]

Many of these colaborers are women serving in seminary, parish ministry, schools, chanceries, hospitals, and beyond. Recent statistics shared by the Center for Applied Research in the Apostolate (CARA) show that there are almost forty thousand lay ecclesial ministers in the United States.[85] They are commonly involved in religious education, sacramental preparation and/or formation, liturgy and/or ministry of music, or general parish administration. Eighty percent of these lay ecclesial ministers are women, with a median age of fifty-five.

In the past decade, the number of female employees working for the pope has increased from 846 in 2013 to 1, 265 in 2023.[86] Whether it be in the parish, chancery offices, schools, seminaries, or leadership at the national or universal level, these women are using their "feminine genius" to serve God's people, forming them as God's sons and daughters—women who bring Mary into pastoral settings and beyond, making her present.[87] In his 1988 apostolic letter, *Mulieris Dignitatem*, John Paul II said:

The Church Listening

The Church gives thanks for *all the manifestations of the feminine "genius"* which have appeared in the course of history, in the midst of all peoples and nations; she gives thanks for all the charisms which the Holy Spirit distributes to women in the history of the people of God, for all the victories which she owes to their faith, hope and charity. She gives thanks for all the fruits of feminine holiness.[88]

Elsewhere, Pope John Paul II remarked that to women "falls the task of being sentinels of the invisible."[89] Interestingly, in his recent Address to the Permanent Deacons of the Diocese of Rome, Pope Francis assigns this very task to permanent deacons when he said, "I expect you to be sentinels: not only to know how to spot the poor in the distant—this is not so difficult—but to help the Christian community recognize Jesus in the poor and the distant, as He knocks on our doors through them."[90] This implies that women, like permanent deacons, are called to be guardians of the Gospel in the world, revealing God's goodness and love to those who are "poor and distant."

The world benefits from this feminine presence and, by extension, seminaries, chancery offices, parishes, and schools benefit from feminine guidance. Similarly, affirming this special sensitivity shown by women, Pope Francis, in a general audience, said that we "have not yet understood in depth what things the feminine genius can give us....It is a path that must be crossed with more creativity and boldness,"[91] implying further study and discernment on the feminine genius will shed light on the path forward for women in ministry.[92]

Similarly, as we have previously discussed, in a recent interview with America Media, Pope Francis affirmed the role of women by declaring the Church to be a "woman," and a "spouse." Here he is implying a mystery, how women are called to "mirror" the Church, in the same way Mary models the

Marian Approaches to Synodality

Church in her perfected state. He went on to say, "We have not developed a theology of women that reflects this."[93] It appears he, like Pope John Paul II, is calling for theologians to tackle this issue.

Moreover, as we heard earlier, in his post-synodal apostolic exhortation on the Amazon, *Querida Amazonia*, Pope Francis affirmed the power of women to make God's love known in families and communities: "The Lord chose to reveal his power and his love through two human faces: the face of his divine Son made man and the face of a creature, a woman, Mary. Women make their contribution to the Church in a way that is properly theirs, by making present the tender strength of Mary, the Mother" (101). Similarly, Leonardo Boff in *The Maternal Face of God* pondered this mystery when he wrote: "If the fact that Mary was a woman has any importance, what face did God wish to show us through the element of the feminine?"[94] Kevin M. Clarke, in his reflection on Mary and God's image, says Mary is a "mediation of an image of the Father...Mary participates in a subordinate way in his (Jesus's) perfect revelation of the Father."[95]

Together men and women image God (Gen 1:27). Mary models this shared humanity, showing how she, precisely as a woman, participates in God's being, mirroring God's love for the world. By extension, women in ministry are called to do the same. Supported by magisterial teaching on lay involvement in ministry, they provide an invaluable service to their communities and beyond as catechists, theologians, and canon lawyers, to name a few examples.

Recently, the Congregation for Divine Worship and the Discipline of the Sacraments acknowledged this outstanding service by all catechists, male and female. With the publication of the Rite of Institution of Catechist, the prefect of this Congregation said the publication "offers a further opportunity for reflection on the theology of ministries in order to arrive at an organic vision of the distinct ministerial realities."[96] Beginning in January of 2022, after episcopal deliberation and planning, laypeople "of profound faith and human maturity" will be instituted using a specific rite of installation as catechists by their bishops during liturgical celebrations, including these words: "Receive this sign of our faith, cathedra of the truth and love of Christ, and proclaim it with your life, your conduct, and your word."[97]

In a *Letter to the Presidents of the Episcopal Conferences on the Rite of Institution of Catechists*, the Congregation for Divine Worship and the Discipline of the Sacraments announced that catechists "by virtue of their Baptism, are called to be coresponsible in the local Church for the proclamation and transmission of the faith, carrying out this role in collaboration with the ordained ministers and under their guidance."[98] Although not exhaustive, the suggested list of ministries associated with the ministry of catechist resemble the tasks associated with a potential "first responder":

> In attempting to offer a by no means exhaustive list of these functions, the following can be indicated: guiding community prayer, especially the Sunday liturgy in the absence of a Priest or Deacon; assisting the sick; leading funeral celebrations; training and guiding other Catechists; coordinating pastoral initiatives; human promotion according to the Church's social doctrine; helping the poor; fostering the relationship between the community and the ordained ministers. (n. 11)[99]

On January 22, 2023, the Catholic News Agency reported that "Pope Francis formally conferred the ministries of lector and catechist upon four men and six women from the Philippines,

Marian Approaches to Synodality

Mexico, Congo, Italy, and the U.K. on Sunday at a Mass in St. Peter's Basilica."[100]

Many celebrate this development as building on a previous step that modified Canon Law on women's access to the ministries of lector and acolyte. Although women have served in these ministries, Pope Francis's *motu proprio* in January of 2021, presents a true and proper institutional mandate, like the instruction of Pope Paul VI in 1972 when he granted access to lay men because they were considered preparation to the eventual admission to holy orders.[101] This means lay ecclesial ministers can now be installed in three major areas of their ministry: lector, acolyte, and catechist, recognizing their ministries as a special office in the Christian community. This previous instruction and these new developments affirm the gifts of lay men and women, showing how the Holy Spirit works through all members of the body of Christ, each with his or her own distinct calling and role.

So, the question becomes, apart from the newly installed ministries, do we need a newly instituted ministry or office to highlight the unique ministry of women? Apart from the great commissioning of Jesus (Matt 28:19–20), does Mary's role in the early Church, well documented in text[102] and liturgical art,[103] a role that inspired other women to evangelize and catechize, call for more discernment and study regarding the role of women in the Church? Moreover, Mary's participation in the priesthood of her son deserves to be included in this discernment, balancing an *ecclesio*-typical approach to Mary, Mary as prototype of the Church, with a *Christo*-typical approach, the analogy between Jesus and Mary. Correspondingly, like Mary, a *pneuma*-typical approach will keep us close to the Holy Spirit, revealing whether we have followed God's will through the experience of the fruits of the Spirit.

This discussion involves men and women, lay and clergy. Additionally, the Document for the Continental Stage affirms

The Church Listening

our common baptismal identity, encouraging us "to participate fully in the life of the Church."[104] The *sensus fidelium* will serve as a barometer for this discernment. The *Vademecum* says:

> The entire People of God shares a common dignity and vocation through Baptism. All of us are called in virtue of our Baptism to be active participants in the life of the Church. In parishes, small Christian communities, lay movements, religious communities, and other forms of communion, women and men, young people and the elderly, are all invited to listen to one another in order to hear the promptings of the Holy Spirit, who comes to guide our human efforts, breathing life and vitality into the Church and leading us into deeper communion for our mission in the world. (1.2)

As members of the Church, we are members of Christ's body, an extension of his work and sacrifice. Mary, too, is connected to this body. Mary is uniquely positioned as having great intimacy with the Holy Spirit and sharing the same flesh with her son. Hence, herein lies the mystery: Have we yet to discern a position for women that honors this connection between Mary and Jesus, their shared humanity? Men and women, by virtue of their baptism, "are formed in the likeness of Christ" (*LG* 7), to be his hands and feet in the world, an extension of his body. Moreover, the magisterium teaches certain men were called to unique missions, namely, the Twelve and their successors, the bishops.[105] Nevertheless, Mary with her "prayerful presence,"[106] and "certain women" were present in the upper room, receiving the anointing of the Holy Spirit at Pentecost (Acts 1:14).

Could it be we haven't given enough attention to this anointing? Could this anointing be considered in the discussion of an institutional expression of the Marian dimension? If yes, would it be seen as a restoration or recovery of Mary's presence in the upper room and standing at the foot of the cross? As mentioned earlier, St. Maximus the Confessor remarked that Mary, the Queen of the Apostles, "held authority: as the Lord did over the twelve disciples and then the seventy, so did the holy mother over the *other women* who accompanied him."[107] Have women looked to Mary's participation in the work of her son as a model for their collaboration with the ministerial priesthood? If a priest acts *in persona Christi Capitis*,[108] can a woman be "another Mary?" What would it mean for a woman to be *in persona Mariae*?[109]

Although all the baptized faithful are "formed in the likeness of Christ" (*LG* 7), as an extension of his body, sharing in his threefold office—prophet, priest, and king—Mary, as model of the Church, invites us to participate in her threefold office: virgin daughter (purity of heart/daughter of Zion); spouse (fidelity); and mother (fruitfulness).[110] If bishops and priests act *in persona Christi*, who represents Mary in a formal capacity? Although a typical response includes the lay faithful as the bride of Christ, the Marian dimension, is it possible to institute a ministry that offers a more formal response?

Apart from the unique pastoral and spiritual activity of the various female religious orders, a new pathway for consecrated and nonconsecrated lay women could serve to further emphasize the complementarity between the successors of the twelve apostles and the apostolic activity of the successors of the early women who ministered to other women. The formation of women ministry leaders, for example, culminating in some sort of installed or instituted ministry, would be one way of restoring the early ministry of women who ministered to women in the early Church.[111]

If the maleness of the apostles in their representation of Christ is used to defend male successors,[112] could not the femaleness of Mary be used to establish a woman as an official "helpmate" or "associate" of a priest? Perhaps leading to the many women who already serve as lay pastoral associates being instituted into a newly installed ministry?

The faithful are asking for some clarity regarding a more formal role for women in the Church, one that recognizes their gifts and contributions made throughout history. Canon law and other Church teachings affirm the gifts and ministries of women. Moreover, certain urgent situations, with the proper permission and training, allow lay men and women to participate in many of the ministries associated with the permanent diaconate. Let us conclude by exploring some options, already mentioned briefly, for a newly installed ministry.

A Newly Installed Ministry: Evangelist

The Lord gives the command; great is the company [*of women*] who bore the tidings. (Ps 68:11)[113] Our study of magisterial texts on the possibilities for lay ecclesial ministry shows the possibility of being appointed as a type of "first responder," as in the case of the Amazon region. As we have seen, it appears the newly installed catechists may serve in this capacity. Nevertheless, bishops' conferences have been entrusted with the task of clarifying roles for the newly installed catechists.[114] Related to this ministry, however, is the call to evangelize, including the possibility of preaching. Although we would need the help of canonists, liturgists, and ecclesiologists to work out the details, we could explore the possibility of addressing these lay preachers with a title like that of "evangelist," a participation in Christ's prophetic office. To be clear, men and women are called to evangelize (*EG* 121). A newly installed ministry, however, although not limited to women, would give women the opportunity to train and use their gifts as lay preachers.

In the early Church, some women belonged to lay ordered ministries, for example, that of virgin or widow.[115] Lynn H.

Marian Approaches to Synodality

Cohick and Amy Brown Hughes, in their book, *Christian Women in the Patristic World*, document the presence of women's offices in the early Church.[116] Similarly, a fourth-century document, *Apostolic Constitutions*, reveals that many of these ministries received some kind of blessing.[117] Installing women in a new ministry would affirm a stable ministry for women, especially for those who have been properly formed, already serving in a variety of ministries. As Pope Francis confirmed in *Querida Amazonia* (99), women have been keeping the faith alive in remote areas of the world. It would be appropriate to honor this service in some official capacity and with a special title. The installation of a new ministry, for example, that of evangelist, to accompany that of catechist, could be considered, assigning women a more formal role in Church ministry. Moreover, they could be trained as preachers, like Hildegard of Bingen who traveled and preached from town to town.[118]

This very issue of women and evangelization was addressed in a key postconciliar document titled "The Role of Women in Evangelization."[119] Published one year after Pope Paul VI's postsynodal apostolic exhortation, "Evangelization in the Modern World" or *Evangleii Nuntiandi*, this mostly forgotten text on the topic of women evangelists acknowledges female biblical figures, including Mary, the mother of Jesus, as "apostles" chosen to "radiate and transmit" the faith:[120]

> All these figures find their highest embodiment in the Virgin Mary, Mother of God, as closely associated as possible with the work of salvation and the spread of the revelation of Jesus Christ, from the Annunciation to the first Pentecost, when Mary, having received the gift of the Holy Spirit, became the Queen of the Apostles, a title which we give her and which is in accord with her nature.[121]

The Church Listening

The document authors go on to recognize the evangelizing efforts of women during and after the Christ event, referring to them as "apostles" who are "among the first models of that female initiative and responsibility" to evangelize. As the first witnesses of the resurrection, they experienced a "foretaste of their apostolic role."[122] Similarly, St. Paul, the apostle to the Gentiles, affirms the ministry of these women in his letters (see Rom 16:1–16). Recall the word *apostle* comes from the Greek *apostolos*, meaning one who is sent to give a message. Moreover, some scholars interpret the word apostle to mean "itinerant preacher."[123] Women, endowed with the gift of faith and the anointing that comes with baptism, are sent to evangelize and care for the people of God.

"The Role of Women in Evangelization," like Pope Francis and his predecessors, affirms the gifts of women in "personal relationships." Living according to the Gospel, they become true witnesses for "if you would preach a sermon, you must yourself be a sermon."[124] This means "no one should evangelize who has not been evangelized and converted."[125]

In the section on women in parishes, it is recommended that women evangelists take on more responsibilities, including more involvement in the apostolate, sharing in those ministries that are not limited to the ministerial priesthood, "a sort of *diaconia*, a service rendered by women."[126] The document ends with a recommendation to look to Mary as inspiration regarding new possibilities for female evangelizers. Consequently, the topic of evangelization, old or first and new, addressed by Vatican Council II in *Ad Gentes Divinitus*, the Decree on Missionary Activity (1965), and Pope Paul VI in *Evangelii Nuntiandi*, continued to be explored and developed in subsequent papal teaching, finding its most recent treatment in Pope Francis's post-synodal apostolic exhortation, *Evangelii Gaudium*, in 2013.[127]

Although the ministry of evangelist, like that of catechist, would not be limited to women, offering some sort of training and formation in this area, followed by some official recognition, would affirm the many women who already serve as evangelists and catechists. On the topic of forming laypeople for ministry, Richard. R. Gaillardetz recommends an "ecclesial re-positioning" that would involve a "personal call, ecclesial discernment and recognition of a genuine charism, formation appropriate to the demands of the ministry, some authorization by community leadership, and some ritualization as a prayer for the assistance of the Holy Spirit and a sending forth on behalf of the community."[128] This process would represent the option of installing a woman in a new ministry, that of evangelist, rooted in the prophetic office of Christ. Some sort of ritual of installation would add meaning and official recognition of the ministry. The same could be considered for women ministry leaders.

Women Ministry Leaders

Earlier in our discernment, we established that the presence of the fruits of the Spirit indicates we are on the right track. Ministries that are led by women are flourishing throughout North America.[129] Women are answering the call to minister to other women, founding their own lay apostolates. Women are acting as spiritual mothers, bringing concerns to the attention of their bishops, who in turn bless their apostolates. Whether they know it or not, as daughters of the Church, not only are they participating in Christ's threefold office, but they are also participating in Mary's threefold office, as living examples of the Church walking together. Although there are many others,[130] I am aware of at least three lay apostolates, founded by women for women that have proven inspirational for others.

With chapters around the world, Magnificat® A Ministry to Catholic Women[131] encourages women to mentor other women, sharing their experiences of faith. Similarly, Dynamic Women of Faith/Catholic Moms Group,[132] founded by Canadian, Dorothy Pilarski, seeks to "connect women with other dynamic women" of faith, including mothers of all ages, allowing them opportunities to learn and grow. Another Canadian woman, Mary Filangi, who founded Women of the Word—Toronto,[133] created a ministry for women, including the power of testimonials, teaching seminars, retreats, conferences, and a referral network for women experiencing vulnerability due to substance use disorders, mental health issues, family life issues, and trauma.

I have been blessed with the opportunity to participate in these thriving ministries, noticing the fruits of the Spirit along the way. Common to these ministries is a strong devotion to Mary. It is no surprise these apostolates are growing, demanding the need for more women trained in this type of ministry. Although the presence of chaplains, or priests, signals the collaboration that is needed to feed the people of God, the presence of these ministries indicates there are some needs that only other women can meet or address. It is not unusual for me to stay behind after having delivered a keynote address, a preached reflection, or a retreat, listening to the stories of mothers, grandmothers, wives, aunts, sisters, and daughters, women of all states of life, with diverse life experiences and personalities, sharing their joys and sorrows, expressing their gratitude that other women are sharing their gifts, inspiring them to do the same. They laugh and cry at my stories, telling me how they see themselves in me and in my life experience. They ask me to pray for them. We must accept that sometimes women prefer to talk to other women, especially regarding sensitive issues.[134] These women inspire me; however, other women who may feel inspired to start a ministry for women may lack formation. Although there are many institutions offering degrees, certificates, and diplomas in lay ecclesial ministry, specialized training in catechesis, preaching, pastoral counseling, music ministry, and retreat ministry would help to form women to minister to other women. Colleges and seminaries could consider creating a certificate or diploma specializing in this ministry led by women.

For many years, the people of God have been discerning a way forward for women. It appears more women are needed to advise the ministerial priesthood on this issue. Moreover, the people of God would benefit from hearing about Mary from a woman's perspective, creating more exposure to women as teachers and preachers.[135] This exposure might lessen the doubt and confusion experienced by some, especially during the synodal process.[136]

On the topic of women and leadership, Sr. Nathalie Becquart, consultor to the General Secretariat of the Synod of Bishops in Rome, remains open to discerning another way of affirming women in ministry: "Maybe the other way is to imagine the Church with another ministerial system, less focused on ordination."[137] It appears she is open to new possibilities for women, showing the need for dialogue and the involvement of women in the discernment process.

The next chapter will show how it is challenging to be of "one mind" on this issue when there is fear, confusion, lack of catechesis, and ambiguity. Moreover, a theology of women must also address other issues that women face that require urgent attention, many of which came up in the synodal consultations. Their voices are key to this discussion. We will address some of these issues in the next chapter. It may take some time to reflect on the needs of women and the global Church, making sure there is unity and clarity. In the meantime, there is enough clarity in magisterial teaching to encourage more leadership roles for women, including the creation of more possibilities for preaching and evangelizing ministries. We have already seen the fruit. It begins with a greater awareness, catechesis, and appreciation of our baptismal priesthood. *We need to know who we are before we can discern and discover what we can do.* Mary, as we have seen, will continue to be an inspiration for

The Church Listening

this discernment. A deeper and richer reflective study on Mary as model of the Church is sure to inform a theology of women.

Mary was an "associate" of Jesus, his helper, participating in his work of redemption. Perhaps our understanding of women's role in the Church will be complete when our understanding of Mary's role in our redemption is complete.[138] This requires further discernment and understanding. We will return to this question in the final, concluding chapter. Leonardo Boff reflects:

> We are probably not far from the day when women will develop a systematic Mariology in light of the feminine as realized both in themselves and, in its perfection, in the Mother of God and our Mother.... If theologians will not assume this task, who will?[139]

4

The Church Understanding

A Marian Approach

To paraphrase popular leadership author Stephen Covey, "we must listen to understand" because all too often, we listen "to respond," without paying attention to someone's context or perspective.[1] Using the account of the wedding at Cana (John 2:1–11), let us consider Mary's gift of understanding as a model for synodal participation. Mary shows how we need people who understand the needs of individuals and families and can address those needs with greater clarity, care, and concern.

In the account of the wedding at Cana, Mary demonstrates this ability to take notice of vulnerability and need. This event marks the first of Jesus's "signs" in the Gospel of John. Jesus and Mary are guests at a wedding in Cana of Galilee when the wine runs out. Without doubt, Mary, sensing the host's reaction to this turn of events, says to Jesus, "They have no wine." As a Jew, she would have known that the groom's family was responsible for providing the wine for the wedding celebration. She tries

The Church Understanding

to spare the family embarrassment, knowing her son could do something about the shortage. Jesus's response to his mother troubles some people: "Woman, what concern is that to you and to me? My hour has not yet come." With the help of commentators, however, the grace in the details comes through, beginning with Jesus's address of "woman" for his mother. In response to the question why does he not call her "mother"? Pope Benedict XVI responds by showing how the title "woman" reveals Mary's contribution to salvation history, expressing "the grandeur of Mary's enduring mission."[2] Kevin M. Clarke, summarizing the thoughts of Pope Benedict XVI, explains:

> "Woman" *points backwards*, as it hearkens to the creation account of Eve, Adam's companion. So here in the account of Cana, Mary represents the companion of the Redeemer. It *points forward* to the Cross, where this "woman" will be made mother in a new way. And it *points to the eschaton*, to the "woman" clothed with the sun. (cf. Rev 11:19 ff.)[3]

Not only does Jesus reveal "the grandeur of Mary's enduring mission," acknowledging her role as a "helpmate" or companion, he reassures her of his divine assistance. Although this may not seem clear without the help of a commentary, scholars who have studied Mediterranean culture in the time of Jesus have discovered the original phrase used by Jesus, "Woman, what concern is that to you and to me?" did not convey disrespect; rather, the phrase was common to Jesus's contemporaries and continues to be used today in everyday conversation in the Middle East. Charles Journet, in his examination of the original phraseology and cultural context, reveals that *"Leave it with me"* is a more accurate rendering of the original expression.[4] Interpreted considering the original language in which the exchange between Mary and Jesus was expressed, Jesus's

Marian Approaches to Synodality

encouraging response to his mother connotes tenderness and intimacy.

Similarly, Sofia Cavalletti, translating the original expression into Italian, concludes that the phrase is best expressed as *nulla ci divide*, meaning "nothing can come between us." She believes this is the correct translation of the phrase uttered by Jesus.[5] This additional context makes sense of Mary's response: "Do whatever he tells you." Mary trusts Jesus and respects his authority, knowing he can do something about the lack of resources.

Adrienne von Speyr, physician and mystic, reflecting on Mary's ability to read vulnerability, remarked, "It is she (Mary), who in the household of the Christianity, will always see where there is lack and where need."[6] Mary's ability to read the room, coupled with her intimacy with her son, moved her to act, to participate and to restore the sense of joy that should accompany a wedding feast. She was not afraid to approach her son, sharing her observation with him.

In this account, we can detect three key Marian movements:

- Mary takes notice of the lack of resources.
- She brings the need to the attention of her son, interceding on behalf of the need.
- She trusts his authority and power to do something about the situation.

Although men and women are called to be nurturing, observant teachers, Mary, representing Church as Mother, identifies the need and brings it to the attention of Jesus, the teacher, showing us how the two models work together. A Marian approach to synodality reproduces this pattern, engaging both models of the Church, that of Mother and Teacher, in the assessment of the needs of the people of God.

The Church Understanding

What Do the People of God Need?

Voices from around the globe responded to the call to participate in synodal consultations. Although the response in some countries was not strong,[7] the *Document for the Continental Stage* reassures the faithful that global "participation exceeded all expectations":[8]

> In all, the Synod Secretariat received contributions from 112 out of 114 Episcopal Conferences and from all the 15 Oriental Catholic Churches, plus reflections from 17 out of 23 dicasteries of the Roman Curia besides those from religious superiors (USG/UISG), from institutes of consecrated life and societies of apostolic life, and from associations and lay movements of the faithful. In addition, over a thousand contributions arrived from individuals and groups as well as insights gathered through social media thanks to the initiative of the "Digital Synod." These materials were distributed to a group of experts: bishops, priests, consecrated men and women, lay men and lay women, from all continents and with very diverse disciplinary expertise. After reading the reports, these experts met for almost two weeks together with the writing group, composed of the General Relator, the Secretary General of the Synod, the Undersecretaries and various officials of the Synod Secretariat, plus members of the Coordinating Committee. This group was finally joined by the members of the General Council. Together they worked in an atmosphere of prayer and discernment to share the fruits of their reading in preparation for the drafting of this *Document for the Continental Stage*. (*DCS* 5)

Marian Approaches to Synodality

The submitted reports shared the concerns and struggles experienced by the people of God. Although there are issues that matter to different groups in different contexts, it is beyond the scope of this chapter to exhaust all issues. Instead, we will focus on a few key issues raised by the syntheses and the *Document for the Continental Stage*, showing how certain women, like Mary, have responded to the needs of people experiencing vulnerability.

In addition to the issue of women in ministry, issues such as impoverishment, violence, discrimination, clergy abuse, homelessness, and immigration were raised by the various syntheses used to inform the writing of the *Document for the Continental Stage* (62, 65). Moreover, many expressed concerns regarding the needs of separated, divorced, and remarried individuals (*DCS* 39), young people (35), people who identify as LGBTQ+, and persons with disabilities.[9] To create a "space for communion, a space for participation, and a foundation for mission," the image of a tent, drawn from the book of Isaiah "Enlarge the space of your tent!" (54:2) was used as a title for the *Document for the Continental Stage* (*DCS* 12). The theme was selected to encourage listening and inclusion:

> (l)istening as openness to welcome: this starts from a desire for radical inclusion—no one is excluded—to be understood in a perspective of communion with sisters and brothers and with our common Father; listening appears here not as an instrumental action, but as the assumption of the basic attitude of a God who listens to his People, as the following of a Lord whom the Gospels constantly present to us in the act of listening to the people who come to him along the roads of the Holy Land; in this sense listening is already mission and proclamation. (*DCS* 11.1)

The Church Understanding

The reports from around the world "give voice to the joys, hopes, sufferings and wounds of Christ's disciples" (*DCS* 15). This means the various drafters of the national syntheses listened to the concerns of the people of God. Like Mary, these individuals reported what they heard from people in their communities, where the need was. They noticed that people need more specialized pastoral care, helping them to feel included and loved. In other words, people experiencing certain vulnerabilities feel exiled and alone. Various syntheses from around the world reported "(t)he dynamic of home and exile, of belonging and exclusion" (*DCS* 29). Clearly, the exclusion of persons leads to exile. By contrast, as I have written elsewhere, the gift of mercy welcomes and heals:

> In his Bull of Indiction declaring the Jubilee Year of Mercy, Pope Francis writes, "We need constantly to contemplate this mystery of mercy. It is a wellspring of joy, serenity and peace. Our salvation depends on it." Pope Francis spoke of this truth in *Evangelii Gaudium* when he affirmed, "The salvation which God offers us is the work of his mercy." This means our divine health (*salus*)—the possibility of divine restoration and deliverance—depends on mercy. Why? It is because the opposite of mercy is emotional, spiritual, and sometimes physical exile. If our spiritual health, our salvation, depends on mercy, the opposite, emotional exile, leads to spiritual illness....If the fruit of mercy consists of joy, serenity, and peace, the fruit of exile is despair, shame, self-loathing, and isolation. Mercy is the end of exile.[10]

Well before the synod on synodality, Pope Francis, in continuity with his predecessors, affirmed the gift of mercy. Sadly, however, the various syntheses are reporting cases where people are experiencing spiritual exile. Shame, feeling bad about oneself, is not a fruit of the Holy Spirit. Rather it robs people of their dignity. Moreover, some people do not feel welcome: "The most common desire in the synodal consultations was to be a more welcoming Church where all members of the People of God can find accompaniment on the journey."[11] The American synthesis noted the tension "between how to walk with people while remaining faithful to the teachings of the Church."[12] The intention is not to change doctrine; rather, the focus is listening, understanding, and discernment.

Recently, this tension provoked the Holy See to issue a statement on the German Synodal Path, *Der Synodale Weg*, a series of conferences or meetings on a variety of issues. Responding to the approach of the German bishops on synodality and their proposals regarding certain issues such as priestly celibacy and governance, women and ordained ministry, same-sex relationships/blessings, and separate and divorced Catholics,[13] the Holy See Press Office issued this statement, in part:

> In order to safeguard the freedom of the People of God and the exercise of the episcopal ministry, it seems necessary to clarify that the "Synodal Way" in Germany does not have the power to compel bishops and the faithful to adopt new forms of governance and new orientations of doctrine and morals. It would not be lawful to initiate in the dioceses, prior to an agreed understanding at the level of the universal Church, new official structures or doctrines, which would constitute a violation of ecclesial communion and a threat to the unity of the Church.[14]

The Vatican News website, reporting on the statement, included the headline: "Germany's Synodal Path Cannot Make Doctrinal Decisions."[15] Consequently, dialogue on the issue of synodal-

The Church Understanding

ity has been strained by the challenge of reconciling doctrine and the need to create awareness regarding the pastoral needs of people experiencing vulnerability and the need for greater collaboration in ministry between men and women. How does the Church maintain unity in doctrine and remain open to the development of a pastoral response to certain situations in need of more specialized care and attention? Will the process of synodality shed some light on how to reconcile this tension? Will the process foster both fidelity to Church teaching and openness to compassionate proposals regarding the care of souls?

Austin Ivereigh, author and commentator, took part in the drafting of the Document of the Continental Stage, working with consecrated persons, clergy, and other laypeople to synthesize the reports gathered from around the world. Although many issues were addressed, most of the document, he says, "is given over not to the issues but to 'process.'" Process, he continues, "is the point of a synod on synodality and it is where the document breaks important new ground by harvesting and giving expression to the desire in the reports for a synodal way of proceeding."[16] The questionnaires presented an opportunity for a global "check-in," allowing the people of God an insight into the joys and sorrows of people from around the world.

The responses varied from synthesis to synthesis, considering the needs and concerns of diverse communities. On some issues, there was no consensus, with extreme responses to the synodal process: "The focus on synodal processes may be frustrating for those impatient to see particular changes that, viewed at least from Manhattan or Munich, seem self-evident. To others who suspect the whole synod process is a dilution or capitulation, it will sound dangerously vulnerable and open-ended."[17] Sr. Nathalie Becquart, aware if this tension, noted the need for global awareness on the topic of women and ministry in the universal Church: "As Western women, we can easily access higher education, but when you look at the situation of women in the world, in many countries many women are still married under 16. That's the reality. In many countries like that, the church is working for the promotion of women, for education. We need to keep that in mind when we look at the global church."[18] Synodal documents, including one of the first continental documents to emerge after the Continental Phase, namely, the *Final Document of the Asian Continental Assembly on Synodality*, comment that issues such as violence against women, lack of education for women, and other forms of oppression must be addressed in our theology of women.[19] Basic human needs are not being met for many women around the world. Notwithstanding the importance of these issues, says Susan Bigelow Reynolds, they should not be used to downplay the need for more women in leadership roles:

> Calls for women's leadership in the Church are frequently miscast as a myopic concern of the West. Not infrequently, the global nature of the Church is cited as reason enough to downplay the urgency of such discussions: *the role of women may be a concern to Catholics in the United States*, the line goes, *but this simply isn't what Catholics in Asia or South America are talking about.* As it turns out, the status of women is very much what Catholics in Asia and South America are talking about. "Almost all reports raise the issue of full and equal participation of women," the *DCS* states.[20]

The discernment process requires mindfulness of the needs of the worldwide Church. Similarly, the Synod Document prepared by the UISG-USG reported wide disparities around the world with women in Africa and some other countries being "excluded from meaningful roles in the Church," where consecrated women are "regarded as cheap labour," even undervaluing "religious life without the habit, without regard for the fundamental equality and dignity of all baptised faithful, women and men."[21] Sadly, these findings echo the situation in India where there have been reports of women religious being exploited and harassed.[22] The discussion on women in ministry requires a listening Church that will pay attention to the living conditions of women around the world. Greater awareness of these issues needs to inform the conversation, helping the Church to address issues that require urgent attention like the discrimination faced by women in some parts of the world. Pope Francis, after his four-day trip to Bahrain in November of 2022, communicated this concern, remarking on the need to treat women as equals to men, denouncing those who treat women as "second class citizens."[23]

With such diverse experiences reported by women from around the world, it is necessary to address their concerns to deepen and clarify our understanding of the role of women in the Church. The only way to handle this tension, says Ivereigh, is to build the "capacity for a synodal church."[24] Clearly, the desire to accompany people needs special attention, including the formation of persons trained to accompany with fidelity and compassion.

Bringing the Needs of the People to the Church as Mother and Teacher

The *North American Final Document for the Continental Stage of the 2021–2024 Synod,* like the *Document for the Continental Stage,* acknowledges the need for more training and pastoral sensitivity when it comes to accompaniment and formation for synodality (21). As the *DCS* states, all people are targeted for this specialized training:

Marian Approaches to Synodality

The overwhelming majority of reports indicate the need to provide for formation in synodality. Structures alone are not enough: there is a need for ongoing formation to support a widespread synodal culture. This formation must articulate itself in relationship to the local context so as to facilitate synodal conversion in the way participation, authority and leadership are exercised in view of more effectively fulfilling the common mission. It is not simply a matter of providing specific technical or methodological skills. Formation for synodality intersects all dimensions of Christian life and can only be *"an integral formation that includes personal, spiritual, theological, social and practical dimensions. For this, a community of reference is essential, because one principle of 'walking together' is the formation of the heart, which transcends concrete knowledge and embraces the whole of life. It is necessary to incorporate in the Christian life a continuous and permanent formation to put synodality into practice, to mature and grow in faith, to participate in public life, to increase the love and participation of the faithful in the Eucharist, to assume stable ministries, to exercise real co-responsibility in the governance of the Church, to dialogue with other Churches and with society in order to bring those who are far away closer in a spirit of fraternity"* (EC Spain). This training will have to be addressed to all members of the People of God: *"For the realization of the said elements of synodality, there is an urgent need for the education and formation programmes for clergy and lay people for developing a shared understanding of synodality that is so vital for journeying together in the local Churches"* (EC Myanmar). In this way, the perspective of synodality will converge with

The Church Understanding

catechesis and pastoral care, helping to keep them anchored in a mission perspective. (82)

The need for greater formation for seminarians and laity emerged in the American and Canadian syntheses, inspiring the call for formation for synodality.[25] Similarly, the *UISG-USG Contribution to the Synod on Synodality* calls for the formation of seminarians or candidates for ordained ministry to be formed "with the capacity for synodality" (VI, 7). Synodality, the report says, "requires a special formation to understand the reality of all the members of the Church: knowledge of cultural, religious, political and social realities, in order to communicate with all" (VI, 7). In other words, what is needed is a multidisciplinary and multidimensional approach to formation, exposing seminarians and others to the realities of the domestic church.

In an article on the topic of human formation, "Discerning a Priestly Vocation: Toward a Program of Integral Human Formation," I proposed a program consisting of various benchmarks for training in human formation, which can be applied easily to laity.[26] Human formation helps individuals cultivate the skills needed to accompany people on the journey toward integration. Although many people acquire these skills in their family of origin, and with the help of good parenting, some people, lacking the necessary supports and resources, are set up in life to be less free to reason and to love, leaving them vulnerable and in need of proper accompaniment.

Sadly, trauma and abuse, too, have lasting effects on individuals, placing limits on freedom and discernment.[27] External chaos risks leading to internal chaos which in turn leads to more external chaos in families, workplace, and the wider community. How can one person accompany another person if they have not addressed their own issues and lack of formation? People need accompanying witnesses, namely, people who mirror integration and restoration.

Marian Approaches to Synodality

In 2016, the Congregation for the Clergy promulgated a new *Ratio Fundamentalis* or method of priestly formation, *The Gift of the Priestly Vocation*, a document addressing today's context further developing the insights of Pope John Paul II found in *Pastores Dabo Vobis* (*PDV*), his "Exhortation on the Formation of Priests in the Circumstances of the Present Day," 1992. The 2016 document highlights the need for every seminary to develop a program of "integrated formation" and personal accompaniment (10, 44). This integrated formation is to lead to "configuration to Christ," meaning the pattern revealed in Jesus is to be reproduced in the life of the priest, a process that begins with our baptism (*PDV* 21). Although neither the *Ratio Fundamentalis* nor *PDV* give any detail regarding the relationship between Mary and seminarians at various stages of their formation, Pope John Paul II did invoke Mary as "Mother and Teacher of our priesthood" and affirms "every aspect of priestly formation can be referred to Mary the human being who has responded better than any other to God's call" (*PDV* 82).[28]

Both magisterial documents, and more recently *Rationes* that have been prepared at the local level,[29] reaffirm four pillars or dimensions of priestly formation: human, spiritual, intellectual, and pastoral. Formation in these four areas contributes to the seminarian's growth, helping him in his discernment. Human formation, however, is the "basis of all priestly formation," cultivating a "series of human qualities" and building the "capacity to relate to others" (*PDV* 43). Each seminary must address this dimension as "the seminarian is called upon to develop his personality, having Christ, the perfect man, as his model and source" (*Ratio Fundamentalis* 93). Although these benchmarks apply to all people, to be configured to Christ the seminarian must, in collaboration with others and God's grace, work on the following human skills: self-knowledge and self-awareness, virtuous leadership, stability of personality or character development, empathy, and self-regulation or self-mastery. In other words, he is called to develop the capacities with which we are endowed by virtue of being created in God's image and likeness, one of the key areas addressed in chapter 2.

In the discussion on the importance of self-awareness and social competencies, the *Ratio Fundamentalis* includes responses to women during the period of discernment. The "ability to relate to women" should be assessed, observing seminarians' interaction with female staff and faculty (*Ratio Fundamentalis* 94). The presence of women in seminary formation, according to the final document of the Australian bishops, assists with this very important work of human formation.[30] Commenting on the pain of the clergy sex-abuse scandal, Jesuit priest, Hans Zollner, agrees with this approach, lamenting the lack of women in seminary formation.

Zollner, director of the Institute of Anthropology Interdisciplinary Studies on Human Dignity and Care at the Pontifical Gregorian University and a former member of the Pontifical Commission for the Protection of Minors, in a webinar on the topic of "Survivor (of clerical abuse) Voices," remarked:

> In the formation setting, the presence of women as counselors, as teachers, and formators is necessary to bring about in males training for the priesthood or *religious life* a much more mature and realistic image and experience of this mysterious human being that is called a woman. Many who trained as seminarians years ago never got any chance to really interact with *women* in a meaningful way.[31]

Zollner went on to call for a new seminary structure, one that allows for more interaction and exposure to human formation. Although he does not offer a "quick fix," he acknowledges the need to form and inform seminarians regarding their own "moral, relational and sexual maturity through normal relationships with families, with women and with children."[32] Hopefully, the meeting of the above identified benchmarks may lead to greater integration and understanding of one's own behavior and the behavior of others. This can only take place with greater humility and self-awareness.

At St. Augustine's Seminary, where I currently serve as assistant dean and associate professor, I created a human formation lecture series, designed to inform seminarians on a variety of topics related to human development. Consequently, our human formation counsellor has noticed an increase in the demand for her counseling services as the topics addressed in the series encourages the men to process their life experiences, especially and including their past hurts and losses. Thankfully, the combination of educational workshops and therapy have proven fruitful. Moreover, the men have appreciated the input and expertise of women accompanying them as they grow and learn.

The virtue of humility, or the habit of knowing the truth about oneself, a key topic covered in my lecture series, is the foundation for good self-knowledge. The *Ratio Fundamentalis* encourages self-awareness because "every seminarian should be aware of his own life history" (94). This knowledge, including knowledge of factors that have influenced behavior and habits, is key to establishing mature and "well-balanced interpersonal relationships" (94).[33] Moreover, "awareness of one's social environment and the capacity for social interaction" (94) hinge on the cultivation of virtuous behavior, the ability to acquire the habits or virtues of self-control, courage, justice, prudence, plus humility and magnanimity. Additionally, perceiving oneself and others correctly informs self-knowledge and virtuous behavior, thereby helping one to feel greater empathy for persons experiencing vulnerability. Clearly, empathy is key to good accompaniment. Sadly, though, some people who have experienced abuse may not be ready to cultivate these skills because they may have been encouraged to suppress their emotions. They need accompanying witnesses to stand with them throughout the process of healing and reconciliation.

Alice Miller, a Swiss psychologist, has researched the pain caused by deficits in the early parent-child relationship, especially the damage caused by fear-based parenting and harsh criticism, preventing a child from expressing emotion in a healthy, life-giving way.[34] Abused individuals, she says, must be given permission to share their "unconscious, repressed hopeless despair," including "feelings of rage, anger, humiliation, despair, helplessness, and sadness."[35] She went on to share her research on early childhood abuse and the damage that ensues with various officials at the Vatican.[36] Although Alice Miller died in 2010, it would take a few years before the issues she raised were addressed with greater empathy and understanding.

In addition to various documents, including a previously unpublished essay by Pope Emeritus Benedict XVI[37] and apologies,[38] Pope Francis has acknowledged the lifelong pain associated with abuse:

> At times, the reality of abuse and its devastating and lasting effects on the life of the "little ones" seem to prevail over the efforts of those who strive to respond with love and understanding. The path to healing is a long and difficult one; it requires firm hope, hope in Christ who went to the cross and even beyond the cross. The risen Jesus bears, and will always bear, the marks of his crucifixion on his glorified body. Those wounds tell us that God saves us not by passing over our sufferings but by *passing through* those sufferings, transforming them by the power of his love. The healing power of the Holy Spirit does not disappoint; God's promise of new life does not fail. We need but

have faith in the risen Jesus and repose our lives in the wounds of his risen body.

Abuse in any form is unacceptable. The sexual abuse of children is particularly grave, as an offence against a life that is just beginning to flower. Instead of flourishing, one who is abused is deeply injured, at times permanently. Recently I received a letter from a father whose son had been abused and as a result for many years could not even leave his room, so profound were the effects of the abuse on him, and on his family as well. Those who were abused sometimes feel, as it were, trapped between life and death. These are realities that, painful as they are, we cannot take away.[39]

Alice Miller, like Mary, approached the teaching Church with a serious concern. She along with other experts and with survivors of abuse have challenged the Church to respond with empathy and a plan of action.[40] Like Miller, these advisors and survivors have sounded the alarm regarding the need for repentance, conversion, transparency, and greater awareness regarding the abuse crisis. To that end, Alice Miller called for "enlightened witnesses"[41] to "provide the mirror,"[42] showing what integration and healing look like. The mirror can be provided by knowing Mary and what it means to develop our God-given capacities with, if needed, the help of pastoral psychotherapy. Hopefully, proper human formation can assist with this process, forming men and women to be accompanying witnesses.

The various issues named in the syntheses and the *Document for the Continental Stage* require accompanying witnesses capable of demonstrating empathy, respect, and concern. Empathy helps with the ability to know the depths of the human heart, "to perceive difficulties and problems, to establish trust

The Church Understanding

in relationships, to listen attentively" (*Ratio Fundamentalis* 94). Empathy, literally meaning "in feeling," allows a person to understand and acknowledge the perspective or feelings of another, to focus on the person, and to restate or affirm what someone is feeling. Empathy encourages the accompanying witness to be attentive to the needs and feelings of others. Moreover, empathy drives accompaniment and informs the pastoral care of people experiencing vulnerability. We mirror Jesus's compassion when we act with empathy.

The Synoptic Gospels contain the account of the healing of Bartimaeus (Mark 10:46–52; Matt 20:29–34; Luke 18:35–43). In Mark's account, Bartimaeus hears Jesus is passing by. He shouts "Jesus, Son of David, have mercy on me!" Sadly, many in the crowd "ordered him to be quiet, but he cried out even more loudly." Moved by his impassioned request, Jesus calls him forward and asks, "What do you want me to do for you?" Bartimaeus asked to be healed of his blindness. Jesus replies, "Go; your faith has made you well," healing him. The synodal process reminds me of this account. There are many in need of mercy and healing, hoping to be noticed, saying, "See me. I'm here. I need help." There may be others, scandalized by vulnerability, not knowing what to do with people experiencing vulnerability, feeling threatened by their call for help. Perhaps, they may be thinking, "what does this mean for the teaching of the Church?" Surely, we cannot order the vulnerable to be quiet. Herein lies the tension, remaining faithful to Church teaching, yet developing a welcoming pastoral response to those people who have been ignored or neglected.

How do we respond to teenagers who are same-sex attracted or identify as LGBTQ+ and are kicked out of their homes, abandoned and rejected by their parents, and now feeling suicidal?[43] How do we accompany a woman who is experiencing poverty, struggling to manage with her five children, after having been beaten, threatened, and abandoned by her

Marian Approaches to Synodality

husband of twenty years? How do we support a young girl who feels self-loathing, comparing herself to others on social media? How do we understand the effects of generational trauma when it comes to victims of abuse, including clergy abuse, or residential school survivors and their offspring? The examples are endless. Trauma-informed education and specialized pastoral care are necessary in these situations.

The issue remains, do these individuals feel welcomed and heard? How many separated and divorced Catholics believe they are not welcomed because they have not been well catechized regarding the teaching of the Church on marriage?[44] Although there are many ministries designed to care for separated and divorced individuals and others experiencing vulnerability,[45] the question remains, do the faithful know about them? How can we create greater awareness? How many received adequate marriage preparation? Elsewhere, I lamented the huge discrepancy between the length of formation for the ministerial priesthood, one sacrament of service (approximately five-to-ten years, depending on diocese or religious order) and approximately one weekend for engaged couples, preparing for the other sacrament of service, marriage.[46] Have our expectations for marriage not taken this lack of formation into account? Have we depended solely on one's family of origin and experience of marriage to inform one's understanding of sacramental marriage? Are we forming clergy and lay ministers for proper accompaniment, using a multidisciplinary approach to human formation and human suffering, teaching ministers how to respond and accompany? Family life is complicated.

During the Synod on the Family, after having heard from experts from around the world on the topic of family life, Pope Francis, like Pope John Paul II in *Familiaris Consortio* (1981), addressed many of these issues in his post-synodal apostolic exhortation *Amoris Laetitia*, On Love in the Family. Pope Francis, raising the need for "new pastoral methods" (199)

The Church Understanding

urged the need for proper accompaniment and preparation for family life. He went on to say, "In the replies given to the worldwide consultation, it became clear that ordained ministers often lack the training needed to deal with the complex problems currently facing families" (202). Pope Francis recommends a "more extensive interdisciplinary, and not merely doctrinal formation in the areas of engagement and marriage" (203). He includes the presence of laypeople, families, and "especially women" in this approach. We need to form ordained and lay ministers for this very important ministry, helping them understand the various factors that influence human behavior: prenatal, postnatal, genetics, family of origin issues, to name a few.[47]

We have spent centuries deepening our understanding of the deposit of faith, bringing clarity and precision where there was ambiguity and confusion. Many ecumenical councils have been called to address disputed issues, leading to the development of doctrinal, legislative, and liturgical/pastoral teaching. The synodal process marks the need to raise awareness of new and sensitive issues and develop pastoral responses. Moreover, following the pattern revealed by Mary, the Church as Mother brings the needs of the people to the Church as Teacher—the magisterium. Thus, Mother and Teacher act in unity. Just as Mary and Jesus acted in unity at the wedding at Cana, communicating with great trust and intimacy, we are called to create more balance and understanding of the Church as Mother and Teacher. We have mastered the model of Teacher; however, the Teacher must listen to the concerns of the Mother, an equally important model for the Church.

Mary brought the needs of her hosts to the attention of her son, knowing he could do something about the lack of resources. The good news is that many faith-filled people are answering the call to formation for accompaniment.[48] The "art of accompaniment" is a significant feature of Pope Francis's pontificate.[49] *The Art of Accompaniment*,[50] a Catholic Apostolate Center resource,

Marian Approaches to Synodality

highlights the need for apprenticeship and learning and forming Christians as missionary disciples. Moreover, the resource lists dimensions of accompaniment, namely,

- Mentoring
- Witnessing
- Spiritual Friendship
- Spiritual Motherhood and Fatherhood[51]

These dimensions are designed to foster a deeper relationship with Christ, leading to greater integration and maturity.

Among many, many others, two examples come to mind of women who have mastered the "art of accompaniment," Sr. Helen Prejean, CSJ, and the Sisters of Life. Sr. Helen Prejean is known as a leading advocate for the abolition of the death penalty. As of 2020, she has accompanied six people to their executions.[52] Not wanting the prisoners to die alone, she accompanied them to their final hour. The 1996 film *Dead Man Walking* is based on her book of the same title, published in 1993. Similar to Sr. Helen's mission to protect the sanctity of life, the Sisters of Life are a community of religious sisters, consecrated women, who have vowed to "protect and enhance the sacredness of every human life."[53] As spiritual mothers, they have helped countless women with crisis pregnancy help, hope and healing after an abortion, retreats, end of life care, and evangelization. Together with Sr. Helen Prejean, they offer a life-giving response to the culture of death and despair.[54]

Clearly, women are answering the call to engage in life-giving ministries, mirroring hope and integration to brothers and sisters in need of healing. These women, modeling synodal accompaniment like Mary, noticed a need in the community, and following the promptings of the Holy Spirit, started something innovative, fostering dialogue and a sense of community.

The Church Understanding

We pray in gratitude for the fruits of the Holy Spirit that are felt by all who encounter them. With Pope St. John Paul II we pray:

> To you, Mother of the human family and of the nations, we confidently entrust the whole of humanity, with its hopes and fears. Do not let it lack the light of true wisdom. Guide its steps in the ways of peace. Enable all to meet Christ, the Way and the Truth and the Life.[55]

5

The Church Acting
A Marian Approach

There is hardly any mention of Mary in the *Document for the Continental Stage*; however, it does refer to Mary as a "missionary disciple."[1] This title is fitting given her intimacy with her son, her accompaniment, and her presence in the upper room before Pentecost: "When they had entered the city, they went to the room upstairs where they were staying....All these were constantly devoting themselves to prayer, together with certain women, including Mary the mother of Jesus" (Acts 1:13–14). This account confirms Mary's presence together with the eleven apostles and "certain women" praying.

The above translation is from the NRSV. Other versions of the Bible include slight variations; for example, the New Jerusalem translation reads: "With *one heart* all these joined constantly in prayer, together with some women, including Mary the mother of Jesus, and with his brothers."[2] The Douay-Rheims version reads: "All these were persevering with *one mind* in prayer with the women, and Mary the mother of Jesus, and with his brethren."[3] Similarly, St. Paul, in his Letter to the Philippians, writes: "Make my joy complete: be of the same mind, having the

The Church Acting

same love, being in full accord and of one mind....Let the same mind be in you that was in Christ Jesus" (Phil 2:2, 5).

The translators of the NRSV preferred the word "together" to communicate the idea of unity. Similarly, the use of the words "one mind" and "one heart" imply unity and harmony. Nevertheless, if we continue to read on in the Acts of the Apostles, it is clear that the early community experienced tension and the threat of division, especially as Paul and other early leaders debated over the issue of Gentile salvation. Additionally, we have examples of certain groups of individuals being of "one mind" or "together" as they planned horrific deeds, namely, the stoning of Stephen in Acts 7:57. Clearly, the obvious distinction here is they did not act of one accord with "the mind of Christ." By contrast, the apostles and early disciples who gathered in Jerusalem to debate the issue of Gentile initiation allowed Paul and Barnabas to share their encounters with Gentiles "as they told of all the signs and wonders that God had done through them among the Gentiles" (Acts 15:12b). Here we have one category or class of apostles, known as "the Twelve," listening to members of another class or category of apostles, namely, Paul and Barnabas. The "whole assembly kept silence, and listened" (Acts 15:12a) as they set out to convince the others that it was not necessary for the Gentiles to convert to Judaism and embrace Jewish customs such as circumcision, for example, before baptism (Acts 15:1). Eventually it was decided that they "should not trouble those Gentiles who are turning to God" (Acts 15:19), agreeing to send others with Paul, accompanying him on his mission to Gentile communities.

This process of discernment, including the desire to ask questions and to listen to the views of others has accompanied the Church throughout the centuries. It was not unusual for ecumenical councils to be called to address a disputed issue, allowing for prayer, study, and discernment to deepen our understanding of a certain revealed truth. At times, the process went on for many years, clarifying ambiguous language, developing doctrine and pastoral and legislative teaching. This process requires humility, attention to detail, dialogue, and closeness to the Holy Spirit. Mary modeled this process in her encounter with the archangel Gabriel: pondering, questioning, and finally accepting or surrendering to the will of God, essentially dialoguing in full freedom. Mary went on to accept her mission, thereby acting in obedience and communion with the Holy Spirit. Moreover, her intimacy with her son gave her the freedom to communicate with him as a loving concerned mother. Similarly, the current process encourages the Church as Mother to speak.

We have already considered the account of the wedding at Cana; however, it was not the first time Mary approached Jesus with concerns. The account of Jesus being lost for three days (Luke 2:51–52) reveals Mary's honesty in her communication with Jesus when she tells him "Child, why have you treated us like this? Look, your father and I have been searching for you in great anxiety" (v. 48). She was free to express her anguish and to ask a question as she did in her encounter with Gabriel. Jesus knew where he was, but she did not. In response, Jesus affirms his identity, declaring he was in his "Father's house." Although confusing to Mary and Joseph (v. 50), the expression of anxiety and the questioning that followed were met with a declaration, affirming his identity, and obedience to his earthly parents. Luke tells us Mary "treasured all these things in her heart" (v. 51). Similar to the scene at Cana, she expressed her concern, listened to her son, and was satisfied with the response. Likewise, the mission of the apostles was clarified after a period of frustration, discussion, questioning, prayer, and openness to listening to the experiences of the others. This gives us hope.

We will know how to act after submitting to the direction of the Holy Spirit, listening with humility and openness. Submission to the power of the Holy Spirit removes the fear from discernment, thereby encouraging us to feel less threatened

The Church Acting

when others express themselves, especially as they share their experiences, hopes and joys. Moreover, the process encourages us to check the fruits of our response. The Synod on Synodality is providing the opportunity for the people of God to share freely their concerns and hopes for the Church. There is a sense of togetherness when the entire people of God is invited to participate.

As we have seen, before the descent of the Holy Spirit, Mary, the apostles, and "certain women" were together in prayer. There was a sense of unity as they comforted one another, constantly praying in preparation for the outpouring of the Holy Spirit promised by Jesus, just before his Ascension (Acts 1:5). Paul followed this practice, encouraging the Thessalonians to "pray without ceasing" (1 Thess 5: 17) in preparation for the second coming of Jesus. The pattern is clear, we cannot stop praying through the discernment. The constant prayer keeps us in communion with the Holy Spirit and with one another.

In another example, after Mary's surrender to the will of God, during her encounter with Elizabeth, she had the courage to recite her song of praise, celebrating the vindication of humble persons who experience divine justice, being filled with "good things" while the proud and corrupt experience retribution (Luke 1:46–55). Mary trusts in God's plan for her life, knowing God will act according to God's mercy and justice. The process of synodality ponders this dynamic, exploring where there is the need for conversion and renewal.

Our sense of mission should reflect this process, especially knowing when to act or not to act, knowing when to walk, knowing when to wait on God or stand. The people of God have been invited to share their concerns and hopes for the Church. The discernment process calls us to pray constantly, reflecting on those issues where there is unity that bears fruit as opposed to unity that destroys, as in the case of the stoning of Stephen. Our unity is fruitful when we think with the mind of Christ, trusting God's will. It will be the fruits of the discernment that will determine whether we are of one mind in Christ. Our baptism reminds us we are sent out to do God's will and to use our gifts as missionary disciples:

> The mission of the Church is realized through the lives of all the baptised. The reports express a deep desire to recognize and reaffirm this common dignity as the basis for the renewal of life and ministries in the Church. (*DCS* 57)

Sadly, however, there are members of the people of God who do not know their common dignity. They have not been formed for discernment. The identity crisis experienced by some members of the Church has made them feel as though they are on the margins or the peripheries. Aware of this experience, Pope Francis encouraged a study on the thoughts and feelings of individuals who feel abandoned or neglected:

> *Doing Theology from the Existential Peripheries* is a research project of the Migrants and Refugees Section (M&R) of the Dicastery for Promoting Integral Human Development, Holy See. It aims at deepening the teaching of Pope Francis and promoting a renewal of theology. The project is built on the belief that those who have been marginalised, whether socioeconomically, socially, or in other ways, hold a wisdom capable of reopening discourse, especially where there are tensions. Specifically, it seeks to uncover the *sensus fidei fidelium* of those often excluded from discourse within society and especially within the Church. In this way, we can nurture and grow Christian thought beginning from a deep

The Church Acting

sense of faith in order to transform lives and hearts once again.[4]

The project team, consisting of theologians and pastoral workers, interviewed 508 people representing forty cities from around the globe. "Through individual interviews and focus groups involving hundreds of women, youth, migrants, people, refugees, prisoners, members of ethnic and cultural minorities, the sick and the differently abled, victims of abuse, and people who have left the Church,"[5] the project team documented the experiences and living conditions of people on the peripheries, culminating in a lengthy report. The results, according to Fr. Stan Chu Ilo, priest and theologian who is a member of the project team, led to the extension of the Synod on Synodality by one year.[6] Accordingly, the North American Synod Team, aware of the needs of people on the peripheries, noted the need for ongoing formation:

> This includes not only formation in the fundamental teachings of our faith, but also formation for synodality, co-responsibility, welcoming, and going out to the peripheries.[7]

Clearly, this marks a desire to listen more intently to the needs of communities from around the world. How would Mary respond to the needs of people experiencing vulnerability? Mary, no stranger to vulnerable situations, had plenty of experiences that connect to the plight of many around the world. Apart from the flight to Egypt where Mary would have experienced the harsh reality of refugees fleeing danger (Matt 2:13–23), the scriptures provide us with two additional examples: her visit with Elizabeth (Luke 1:39–56), representing scenarios where we are called to walk, and her standing at the foot of the cross (John 19:25–27), representing scenarios in which we are called to accompany and be still with persons experiencing vulnerability. Each example demonstrates a way of responding pastorally to people in need of accompaniment. The synodal process has shed light on the needs and concerns of the people of God, encouraging discernment regarding the correct pastoral response. Apart from Mary's accompanying intercessory prayer, Mary's earthly activity provides a framework for such a response.

A Marian Style of Accompanying: Mary Goes to Elizabeth

Reflecting on Mary's visit to Elizabeth, *Towards a Spirituality for Synodality* tells us that

> Mary and Elizabeth anticipate the prophetic Church. Their presence reminds it that it speaks best when it speaks from its experience of God's grace in its own life. In Mary's journey to her kinswoman Elizabeth and Elizabeth's response, we are shown the way to a synodal community of welcome, refuge, and joy. In them, we learn that from listening to the Word comes receiving and welcoming the unexpected gift of God, for whom nothing is impossible. Together, Mary and Elizabeth, and all the generations which enter their song, are already the community of hope that God's promises in Christ will never fail. (49)

In Luke's Gospel, the archangel Gabriel tells Mary that her relative Elizabeth has conceived a son (Luke 1:36). Upon hearing the news, Mary "set out and went with haste" to visit with Elizabeth (Luke 1:39). Mary, like the Good Shepherd, leaves her community to support a loved one in need. She models for us

The Church Acting

Pope Francis's vision of a "church that goes" to encounter the other.[8] For three months, Mary accompanies her relative, supporting her and, without doubt, delighting in life-giving conversation. Her visit with Elizabeth reveals three key actions needed in our synodal efforts:

- Go to the person in need.
- Recognize the dignity of the other person.
- Allow the experience of the other to influence you.

Mary visits her relative Elizabeth, marking the celebration of two miraculous pregnancies. Elizabeth and Zechariah had struggled with infertility for a long time; now they are ecstatic that Elizabeth is with child for "nothing will be impossible with God" (Luke 1:37). Similarly, Mary, still pondering the revelation regarding the identity of her own son, rejoices in her news. She goes to Elizabeth, supporting her in her time of need and preparation.

The great gift of this visit, a mystery of our faith, is the exchange between Elizabeth and Mary. Elizabeth's extraordinary greeting, like that of the archangel Gabriel, finds its way into the Hail Mary: "Blessed are you among women and blessed is the fruit of your womb" (Luke 1:42). Elizabeth, "filled with the Holy Spirit" (Luke 1:41), knows Mary is "blessed among women" and knows her child is blessed. This exchange, explains Dr. Matthia Langone, iconographer and professor, is the mystery revealed in the encounter. The visit, she says, is not the mystery; the mystery is Elizabeth's recognition of Mary as mother of the Messiah and John the Baptist's recognition of the presence of Jesus in Mary's womb.[9]

This encounter marks a deep recognition between two individuals filled with the Holy Spirit, the power of God's love. This type of familiar resemblance transcends blood ties. It is the presence of the Holy Spirit that one recognizes in the other. One of the greatest gifts a missionary disciple can give another person is the gift of recognition, communicating the identity of the human person, as a person with dignity, created in the image of God. Elizabeth's declaration affirms Mary's identity and her mission—she is blessed among women. Inspired by the Holy Spirit, Elizabeth's words show she knows Mary's identity and is aware that Mary has been set apart for this great mission. Mary responds to this recognition with great delight when she sings her song of praise (Luke 1:46–55). When our love for others is free of fear, we participate in God's love for people because we are free to see them as beloved children of God.

Nevertheless, what is remarkable about this mystery of our faith is that Mary "sets out and went with haste" (Luke 1:39) to accompany her relative, perhaps thinking she was the one expected to give time and energy to her loved one, only to be comforted and inspired by Elizabeth's gift of recognition, confirming her sense of mission, and making her feel supported and known. Even though this text is a celebration of the good news shared by Mary and Elizabeth, apart from assisting Elizabeth, I often wonder whether Mary, aware of her own needs, went to visit Elizabeth for comfort and respite.

In Matthew's Gospel, we hear that Joseph did not believe Mary's story and was tempted to abandon her. Matthew's account, however, does not tell us how much time elapsed between Joseph's doubt or potential rejection, and his dream, when he is reassured that Mary did not betray him. All we hear is that "just when he had resolved to do this (dismiss her quietly), an angel of the Lord appeared to him in a dream and said, 'Joseph, son of David, do not be afraid to take Mary as your wife, for the child conceived in her is from the Holy Spirit'" (Matt 1:20). Is the purpose of Mary's visit to support Elizabeth? Or is it *also* about her need for emotional and spiritual support? Was she pondering Joseph's initial reaction, needing someone

The Church Acting

like Elizabeth to affirm her mission, believing her good news? Inspired by the message in his dream, Joseph awakens from his physical and spiritual sleep, reassured of Mary's goodness. I have often wondered whether this awakening coincided with Mary's return from her visit with Elizabeth.

What message is revealed here regarding a Marian approach to synodality? Not only did Mary walk with Elizabeth, showing her support during the final months of her pregnancy, but Elizabeth also walked with Mary, affirming her identity and mission, bringing her comfort during a time of unknowns, especially, perhaps, waiting for Joseph to believe her news regarding her miraculous pregnancy. Mary represents the one who walks with those requiring assistance with daily needs, and Elizabeth represents the one who walks with someone who may need some refuge, a break from gossip, slander, and misunderstanding.[10]

Applying this to the synodal process, it means the one who goes out to the peripheries to listen, to understand, and to accompany those experiencing vulnerability must remain open to the possibility of learning new things about themselves and receiving from the other the gift of affirmation or some other remarkable insight into the human experience. It is a gift of mutual recognition. Hence, we must open ourselves to the possibility of learning from others. This was the experience of members of the project team that prepared the lengthy report for the Dicastery for Promoting Integral Human Development, sharing their learning and insights during the conference Doing Theology from the Peripheries, held in Toronto in November of 2022:

> In the course of our encounter with people, I learned, for instance, at the African American parish in Chicago, St. Agatha, of the terrible isolation and alienation many African American seniors felt during the pandemic. I heard of the pain and abandonment

Marian Approaches to Synodality

many Catholics felt during the Eucharistic desert occasioned by the COVID pandemic. Many parishes were being permanently closed in African American neighborhoods, and people are hurting from being discarded because of socio-economic status and racism. I heard of some Catholics who left the church and joined new Pentecostal movements, abandoning the practice of faith and becoming hostile to the Church.[11]

Fr. Stan Chu Ilo, the source for the above quote, was enriched by his encounter with those considered "outside the walls." More and more, we are hearing about the fallout from severe pandemic lockdowns; for example, in my hometown, suicide attempts among young people tripled during lockdown.[12] Moreover, substance use disorder doubled, and eating disorders increased by 90 percent.[13] Sadly, some of these young people felt lost and alone. Hearing about these experiences should deepen our understanding of the need to listen, act, and walk with those experiencing vulnerability. Although during lockdown many felt lost inside the walls, like the coin in the Parable of the Lost Coin (Luke 15:8–10), Mary, like the woman who searches for the lost coin, provides a model for how to walk and stand with those considered "outside the walls."

This recalls the account of Hagar and Ishmael in the Book of Genesis. Hagar, Abraham's servant, gives birth to Ishmael, his first son. When tensions arise between Hagar and Sarah, Abraham's legal wife, and Ishmael and Isaac, his legal son, Hagar and Ishmael are banished. While wandering to find a home, she refers to God as the "Living One Who Sees Me" (Gen 16:14). This insight reminds us of Elizabeth who sees Mary, and Mary, like our Living God, who sees the suffering of her son and stands with him, thereby modeling pastoral accompaniment.

The Church Acting

Marian Synodality: Mary Stands with Jesus "Outside the Walls"

> So they took Jesus; and carrying the cross by himself, he went out to what is called the Place of the Skull, which in Hebrew is called Golgotha. There they crucified him, and with him two others, one on either side, with Jesus between them. (John 19:16b–18; cf. Mark 15:22)

The Letter to the Hebrews adds some context to the scene of the crucifixion: "For the bodies of those animals whose blood is brought into the sanctuary by the high priest as a sacrifice for sin are burned outside the camp. Therefore, Jesus also suffered outside the city gate in order to sanctify the people by his own blood. Let us go to him outside the camp and bear the abuse he endured" (Heb 13:11–13). The author of the Letter to the Hebrews is aware of the teaching found in Leviticus regarding the handling of the unclean (14:33–45) and the slaughtering of animals in or outside the camp (17:3). Fr. Stan Chu Ilo used this image to capture the experience of people on the peripheries:

> We must remember that Jesus was killed outside the wall of the city. It was outside the walls of Jerusalem, the big city, that our redemption was wrought. Perhaps, it is in going outside the cities, outside our churches, traversing and breaking these walls that we can find the Savior again hanging on the tree and calling us to life and freedom and welcoming us to the bosom of God's infinite and inclusive divine love.[14]

Similarly, the author of the Letter to the Hebrews invites us to go "outside the camp" to live and serve like Jesus. Mary knew this experience well, standing with her son during his deepest agony.

Marian Approaches to Synodality

Dietrich Bonhoeffer (1906–45), martyred during World War II, reflected on the pain of public humiliation in his *Meditations on the Cross*. Focusing on themes of cross and resurrection, suffering and death, he pondered the scene in which Jesus died:

> It is infinitely easier to suffer in obedience to a human order than in the freedom of one's own, personal, responsible deed. It is infinitely easier to suffer in company than alone. It is infinitely easier to suffer publicly and with honor than out of the public eye and in disgrace. It is infinitely easier to suffer through the engagement of one's physical being than through the Spirit. Christ suffered in freedom, alone, and out of the public eye…in body and soul, and likewise subsequently many Christians along with him.[15]

Jesus's *kenosis*, or self-emptying (see Phil 2:5–8), meant he did not use his divine powers for personal gain. By assuming our humanity, he agreed to laugh and cry like us and to live and die like us, experiencing as Bonhoeffer says, "debasement, revilement, persecution" and the pain of being misunderstood.[16] Similarly, Mary, his mother, would have suffered these offenses with him, hearing all the gossip and the threats, which tore at her heart:

> At the foot of the cross, from her suffering son and Lord, her mission is confirmed: to be the mother of the new community born from his sacrifice. At the foot of the cross, gathered with her community of faithful women bound in love and friendship beyond the natural bonds of family, we find her. Together, they are not afraid to be seen as those who love him; to bear witness to him when all have deserted and are

filled with fear. Through their long vigil of his suffering, putting their own lives at risk, they show a love that is stronger and more enduring than any worldly power. With these women, Mary waits to receive the tortured and lifeless body of her son into her arms and place him in the tomb, returning him to the Father God who gave him to her.[17]

Mary's experience during this encounter reveals a model for standing with those "outside the walls":

- She goes with Jesus "outside the walls."
- She stays with Jesus, standing at the foot of the cross.
- She becomes our mother, standing with us, modeling how to be a Church that stands together.

John's Gospel includes a moving moment, another mystery, between Jesus on the cross and his mother, standing at the foot of the cross with Mary, the wife of Clopas, Mary Magdalene, and John, the beloved disciple: "When Jesus saw his mother and the disciple whom he loved standing beside her, he said to his mother, 'Woman, here is your son.' Then he said to the disciple, 'Here is your mother'" (John 19:26–27a). Of this moment, Pope Benedict XVI says, "Mary has truly become the mother of all believers."[18] In her suffering, she embraces more children, showing us how to be loving and fruitful with our joys and sorrows. She did not allow fear or thoughts of self-preservation to keep her from accompanying her son, key insights shared by Martin Luther King, Jr., during his last speech before his death in 1968, "I've Been to the Mountaintop."

Reflecting on the Parable of the Good Samaritan in Luke's Gospel (10:25–37), King shares some context and insights inspired by a trip to the Holy Land, remarking how he came to see that the road to Jericho is "conducive for ambushing."[19] He provides an interesting perspective as to why the priest and the Levite do not stop to help the man beaten by thieves and abandoned on the road to Jericho. Although some, he says, believe they didn't stop due to laws pertaining to ritual cleanliness, he believes they failed to stop and help the man due to fear and the desire for self-preservation. The priest and Levite, he believes, thought "If I stop to help this man, **what will happen to me**?" Their fear of being ambushed by the same thieves, he says, prevented them from stopping. Sadly, fear, the emotional response to threat, real or imagined, can keep us from being merciful. The Good Samaritan, however, according to King, thought to himself, "If I do not stop and help this man, **what will happen to him**?" Clearly, the Good Samaritan, like Mary, modeled pastoral accompaniment—the courage to risk suffering, to the point of offering to sacrifice one's comfort and safety to walk with another in their time of pain.

Mary empties herself during this painful ordeal, having given a total gift of self to God and God's plan for our salvation; she now stands in agony as her son, the source of our salvation, dies before her, painfully public with her sorrow, possibly standing as a widow, since Joseph's presence is not recorded in any crucifixion scene of the New Testament. Pope John Paul II believes this is the deepest gift of self in human history.[20]

Mary stands with everyone who experiences gossip, slander, or threats, exiled to the peripheries. She knows the pain of a parent whose child awaits trial, how long and agonizing the time is as one awaits one's fate. Likewise, she stands with everyone who has experienced trauma, or witnessed the loss of a loved one, especially a tragic, violent end of life. When someone is taken from us prematurely, or due to the sins of others, such as through an act of violence, we find ourselves in shock, disillusioned. Mary is left in the land of the living with her own emotional crucifixion. "And a sword will pierce your own soul

The Church Acting

too," Simeon said to her at the presentation in the temple (Luke 2:35b), foreshadowing the agony associated with the loss of her son.[21]

As we heard earlier, Mary's loss of her son, according to Maximus the Confessor, is a "second offering" to God.[22] Hence, there is a double offering: Mary offers her suffering to God and offers, with God, her son for our salvation. As we have seen, this offering inspired St. Ignatius of Loyola and John Paul II to believe Mary is present at every Mass with us,[23] standing with us, reminding us we are not alone as we offer up our own struggles.

John Paul II concluded his apostolic letter *Salvifici Doloris* (On the Christian Meaning of Human Suffering), with an appeal to stand with Mary, "who stood beneath the cross." Just as Mary stood with her son, we, too, he says, are called to see Jesus in the suffering of others: "He himself is present in this suffering person," and all "who suffer have been called once and for all to become sharers 'in Christ's sufferings.'"[24] Hence, like Mary, we are called to be "participants of the divine nature" (2 Pet 1:4) and "sharers in Christ's sufferings" (1 Pet 4:13). Mary, revealing the pattern that is to be reproduced in us, shows us we cannot be one without the other.

In a mysterious way, Mary remains with us, praying for us, accompanying us as we strive for holiness and healing. She, the accompanying witness, suffers with us as she suffered with her son. She models for us the intimacy that is required in accompaniment, guiding the synodal path. Fearlessly standing with people "outside the walls," or inside prison walls as does Sr. Helen Prejean, CSJ, a tireless defender of life, we are called to communicate our care for others with compassion and empathy, giving people hope for redemption and healing. Standing with people reminds them they are not alone in their crisis, giving them hope to recover and find new life in Christ, or, as in the case of Sr. Helen Prejean, bringing them comfort and reminding them of God's mercy in their final hour. Intimacy with Mary helps with this journey.

Pope Benedict XVI reflected on the need for intimacy with Mary in his catechesis on the connection between Mary and the priesthood. Of this he said "sacrifice, priesthood and Incarnation go together, and Mary is at the heart of this mystery."[25] Using the foot of the cross as an example, he contextualizes the words of Jesus to his mother and the beloved disciple John by going back to the Greek text:

> The Gospel tells us that from that hour St. John, the beloved son, took his mother Mary "to his home." This is what it says in the English translation; but the Greek text is far deeper, far richer. We could translate it: he took Mary into his inner life, his inner being, "*eis tà idia*," into the depths of his being. To take Mary with one means to introduce her into the dynamism of one's entire existence it is not something external and into all that constitutes the horizon of one's own apostolate.[26]

This means contemplating Mary involves intimacy with her, trusting in her maternal intercession and welcoming her into our very being.

Mary's standing with her son and with his followers inspires us to think of those in the peripheries, or those hidden among us, too afraid to ask for help. Like Simeon, Mary "saw salvation" in her son. She knows what restoration and integration look like. Being called to be *stand-ins* for Mary in today's world involves the ability to mirror integration and the possibility of healing, especially for those in exile. Chapter 3 of this study proposed ways in which women are standing in or can stand in for Mary in these contexts. The presence of these women is an extension of Mary's presence, beyond representations in liturgical art, as beautiful and enriching as they are. They are spiritual mothers accompanying God's children, reminding them they are not alone. Pope Benedict XVI reminds us that

> Mary is the Spiritual Mother of all humanity, because Jesus on the Cross shed his blood for all of us and from the Cross he entrusted us all to her maternal care.[27]

6

Mary
Our Model for Synodality

Throughout this study, we have considered what it means to adapt a Marian style of synodality. We have examined Mary's life, her response to suffering, and her collaboration with her son, Jesus. We reflected on Mary's role in the life of the Church:

- Mary as Model of the Church (mission)
- Mary and the Holy Spirit (participation)
- Mary and her son, Jesus (communion)

Moreover, we have observed how Mary is the first participant or sharer in at least four areas of Jesus's life:

- First participant in the divine nature
- First participant in the sufferings of Christ
- First participant in the one priesthood of Christ
- First participant in the mission of Christ

We have seen how she pondered, questioned, and surrendered to God's plan for her life, ultimately saying yes to God's will.

Mary

We applied this framework to the current discussion on women in ministry, helping us to discern a path forward for women. Moreover, we have affirmed her ability to recognize need in the community, as in the case at the wedding at Cana, bringing it to the attention of her son, knowing he could do something about the lack of resources, and ultimately deferring to his authority. This intimate exchange with her son revealed a unique insight into the models of Church as Mother and Teacher, a Church that recognizes need, addresses that need, and forms her sons and daughters to minister to the people of God.

We celebrated her desire to assist her relative Elizabeth, only to be affirmed and comforted herself, culminating in a beautiful mutual recognition of the presence of the Holy Spirit in the other. This delightful encounter signals the possibility of being transformed and affirmed in our ministry to others, especially revealing how ministry can be mutually satisfying. Finally, we pondered the mystery of Jesus's death, how Mary going with him "outside the walls" and standing with him reveal the pattern to be reproduced as we walk with others, especially with those on the peripheries. We have discerned with Mary, seeing how the experience of the fruits of the Holy Spirit confirm we are on the right path, signifying unity. Moreover, we have considered what it means to walk and stand with the people of God. The following chart summarizes a proposed Marian style of synodality.

Table 3. A Marian Style of Synodality	
Listening —The annunciation	· Ponder issues without fear. · With sincerity, question and study revealed data. · Submit to the Holy Spirit with prayer and discernment and the help of the sacraments. · Acknowledge the fruits of the Spirit as confirmation. · Trust and obey God's plan.

Continued

Marian Approaches to Synodality

Understanding —The wedding at Cana	· Assess need in the community. · Identify need. · Bring it to the attention of those who can address the need, including the formation of individuals for service and accompaniment.
Acting —Pentecost —The visitation —John's account of the death of Jesus	· Go to the persons experiencing vulnerability, "outside the walls." · Be open to learning something about yourself. · Stand with people, accompanying them in their time of need.

This Marian framework could be used to develop a pastoral response to those experiencing vulnerability or those searching for answers regarding God's plan for their lives. It is a model of accompaniment. **Mary models how Jesus wants us to stay or remain in a relationship with him (John 15:4).** As we have seen, walking and standing together, according to St. John Chrysostom, describes the activity of the Church.[1] Moreover, Jesus, in the account of the journey to Emmaus (Luke 24:13–35), walks and dialogues with two disciples, listening, questioning, talking, and revealing God's glory and truth to them. This walking together is meant to inspire listening and learning:

> We recall that the purpose of the synod, and therefore this consultation, is not to produce documents, but "to plant dreams, draw up wounds, weave together relationships, awaken a dawn of hope, learn from one another and create a bright resourcefulness that will enlighten minds, warm hearts, give strength to our hands."[2]

Although the Preparatory Document for the Synod on Synodality clarifies the purpose of the Synod as not producing documents, some may fear the outcome of the process, believing the pastoral response implied in the process will lead to change in doctrine. Jos Moons, in an article on synodality, says the anointing of the Holy Spirit will accompany the process, concluding that the virtue of obedience, "including the submission that goes with it, does not disappear."[3]

Although the synodal process allows for dialogue and questioning, a final word may be required on behalf of the magisterium "that participants need to obey. A synodal process cannot exist without participants accepting a final decision."[4] This means responses will be recognized and acknowledged, but only truth will be affirmed. It is in this way that the synod participants will be following a Marian style of synodality, obeying the promptings of the Holy Spirit. Like Mary, we must remain intimately connected to the Holy Spirit, checking always for the fruits of the Spirit (Gal 5:22–23).

Pope Francis praised this Marian style in *Evangelii Gaudium*, a document linking evangelization with accompaniment, emphasizing Mary's love and tenderness and her knowledge of God's justice and mercy (*EG* 288). Without Mary as the "Star of the New Evangelization,"[5] Pope Francis writes, we never "truly understand the spirit of the new evangelization" (*EG* 284). Mary reveals the path forward, leading to Jesus and the truth, especially and including the path forward for women in ministry, creating "still broader opportunities for a more incisive female presence in the Church" (*EG* 103). Perhaps, as hinted at the end of chapter 3, a more incisive role for women may be uncovered after our understanding of Mary's role in salvation history is complete.

A Fifth Marian Dogma?

Mary's *fiat* has inspired countless reflections, encouraging many to ponder the significance of her participation in her son's redeeming activity, including the decades-long discussion regarding the proposal of a fifth Marian dogma, Mary as "co-redemptrix" with Jesus.[6]

While it is beyond the scope of this final and concluding chapter to enter into any great detail regarding this issue, it is relevant to this discussion and deserves some attention. This idea was discussed just before the gathering of bishops at the Second Vatican Council, including a preparatory study on Mary that was circulated before the Second Vatican Council.[7] Almost 600 of the Council participants requested a discussion on Mariology. Roughly 400 wanted some clarification regarding Mary's mediation, and 250 wanted a dogmatic definition deepening our understanding of Mary's participation in our redemption.[8] Although many supported a separate document on Mary, meaning there would have been seventeen documents instead of sixteen, it was decided to include Mary within the Dogmatic Constitution on the Church, *Lumen Gentium*, chapter 8. No solemn declaration was made regarding Mary's mediation; however, Mary's unique participation in Jesus's act of redemption was affirmed (*LG* 56, 58, 61). This means; however, **Mary's participation is subordinate to the work of Jesus Christ, our redeemer**. Concerning the matter of Mary's maternal mediation, Pope John Paul II writes:

> Mary's maternal mediation does not obscure the unique and perfect mediation of Christ. Indeed, after calling Mary "Mediatrix," the Council is careful to explain that this "neither takes away anything from nor adds anything to the dignity and efficacy of Christ the one Mediator" (*LG* 62). And on this subject it quotes the famous text from the First Letter to Timothy: "For there is one God and there is one mediator between God and men, the man Christ Jesus, who gave himself as a ransom for all." (2:5–6)[9]

Mary

Mary's obedience at the annunciation (Luke 1:38) and her suffering with her son at the foot of the cross (John 19:25–27) are often cited as support for the proposed Marian dogma of coredemption. Sadly, however, some of the confusion around this proposed dogma surrounds language. It is important to note that the prefix "co" derived from the Latin "*cum*" means "with" and not "equal."[10] Although Mary has been invoked with the title coredemptrix,[11] our understanding of her contribution to our redemption has not been deepened or proclaimed by a solemn act of the magisterium. Marian dogma, according to some scholars, "will not be complete until the Church presents a dogma directly defining the nature of Mary's coredemptive mission with the Redeemer."[12] To be clear, the proposed fifth dogma was not defined at the Council; however, as we have seen in chapter 2, it did refer to Mary as Mediatrix and Advocate (*LG* 62), reminding the faithful of the power of her maternal intercession and her intimacy with the Holy Spirit, also referred to as Advocate.

The Council fathers acknowledged Mary as "suffering grievously with her Son" (*LG* 58) and noted the reality of participatory mediation: "The unique mediation of the Redeemer does not exclude but rather gives rise to a manifold cooperation which is but a sharing in the one source" (*LG* 62). Moreover, Mary, as an associate, is affirmed for her cooperation in the work of salvation (*LG* 56). The Council fathers are not alone in their affirmation of Mary's participatory mediation.[13]

In 1918, in an encyclical, Pope Benedict XV declared, "She [Mary] may rightly be said to have redeemed the human race together with Christ."[14] Similarly, Pope Pius XI, in a 1935 radio message to Lourdes, referred to Mary as "co-redemptrix" at least five times.[15] Not only do several early Christian writers refer to Mary's unique cooperation,[16] but Pope John Paul II used the term "co-redemptrix" at least seven times.[17] Moreover, the world-renowned Mariologist, René Laurentin, although not convinced of the need for a proposal for a fifth Marian dogma, believed Mary "cooperated with the unique Redemption on a supreme level and with a unique intimacy."[18] Although Pope Benedict XVI resisted using the term "co-redemptrix,"[19] he did acknowledge how Mary, "who with her 'yes' made possible the gift of Redemption."[20] Clearly, Mary's role as "helpmate" or "associate" is affirmed in these reflections.

A request for Pope Francis to grant public recognition and honor "to the role of the Blessed Virgin Mary for her unique human cooperation with the one divine Redeemer in the work of Redemption as "**Co-redemptrix with Jesus the Redeemer**"[21] was submitted on January 1, 2017, by the International Marian Association in the document, *The Role of Mary in Redemption*. The document ends with the following:

> Therefore, we, as members of the Theological Commission of the International Marian Association, and in full obedience and fidelity to our Holy Father, Pope Francis, humbly request that during this 2017 Fatima centenary, and in continuity with the papal precedents of Pope Pius XI and Pope St. John Paul II, Pope Francis would kindly grant public recognition and honor to the role of the Blessed Virgin Mary for her unique human cooperation with the one divine Redeemer in the work of Redemption as **"Co-redemptrix with Jesus the Redeemer."** We believe that a public acknowledgement of Mary's true and continuous role with Jesus in the saving work of Redemption would justly celebrate the role of humanity in God's saving plan and lead to the release of historic graces through an even more powerful exercise of Our Lady's maternal roles of intercession for the Church and for all humanity today.

Mary

These titles imply that Mary shared in Jesus's authority, shedding light on the "profound yet complementary" link between the Marian and Petrine dimensions. It is this insight that deserves more attention when it comes to our discernment regarding a theology of women—a theology of women as associates when it comes to collaboration in ministry. Moreover, there is another link between Jesus's redeeming activity and Mary's cooperation. It is found in the Book of Genesis and later affirmed in the Gospel of Luke.

Elizabeth's extraordinary greeting, "Blessed are you among women and blessed is the fruit of your womb" (Luke 1:42), is loaded with meaning. Two other women were considered blessed among women in sacred scripture: Jael in the Book of Judges (5:24) and Deborah in the Book of Judith (13:18). Edward Sri explains that these women were considered blessed

> because the Lord used them to rescue the people from their enemies....Mary also shares with Jael and Judith a common association with the imagery of Genesis 3:15. Jael and Judith are blessed among women because they struck the heads of their enemies. This recalls the imagery foreshadowing the future Messiah.[22]

Genesis 3:15 reads as follows: "I will put enmity between you and the woman, and between your offspring and hers; he will strike your head, and you will strike his heel." The context for this verse is the aftermath of the Fall; God reveals the first Messianic prophecy, addressing first the serpent in 3:14–15, followed by the woman and the man. The prophecy indicates there will be hostility or enmity between the evil one and the woman, suggesting the presence of evil whenever and wherever women are oppressed and abused. What is striking, however, is the version of 3:15 found in the Vulgate, the classical Latin translation of the Bible, where the female pronoun is used for the one who strikes or crushes the head of the enemy: "I will put enmities between thee and the woman, and thy seed and her seed: *she* shall crush thy head, and thou shalt lie in wait for *her* heel."[23]

Liturgical images of Mary crushing the head of the serpent abound because of the early influence of this translation.[24] Moreover, this detail is noteworthy, especially because Our Lady of Guadalupe, in her exchange with St. Juan Diego, reveals herself as "the one who crushes the head of the serpent," *Coatlaxopeuh*, later translated as Guadalupe. Regardless of the use of the male or female pronoun for Genesis 3:15, both are theologically correct. Jesus crushes evil thereby accomplishing our redemption, and Mary, with her cooperation, crushes evil with her receptivity to the promptings of the Holy Spirit and her humility. In effect, she is a *cocrusher of evil*. St. Augustine, aware of Mary's role in salvation history, in his work *The Christian Combat*, emphasized how God's plan for our salvation included Mary's participation:

> The Lord Jesus Christ, having come to liberate human beings, including both men and women destined for salvation, was not ashamed of the male nature, for He took it upon Himself; or of the female, for He was born of a woman. Besides, there is the profound mystery that, as death had befallen us through a woman, Life should be born to us through a woman. By this defeat, the Devil would be tormented over the thought of both sexes, male and female, because he had taken delight in the defection of them both. The freeing of both sexes would not have been so severe a penalty for the Devil, unless we were also liberated by the agency of both sexes.[25]

Mary

Mary participates in Jesus's act of conquering evil. St. Paul, familiar with the messianic prophecy of Genesis 3:15 and the act of crushing evil, encouraged Christians living in Rome when he wrote, "The God of peace will shortly crush Satan under your feet" (Rom 16:20). We, like Mary, are called to be cocrushers of evil. This important detail must be considered in the discussion regarding Mary as coredeemer.

Even though, as of this writing, no formal response to the International Marian Association has come from Pope Francis, in a homily on April 3, 2020, he said:

> Our Lady did not want to take away any title from Jesus; she received the gift of being His Mother and the duty to accompany us as Mother, to be our Mother. She did not ask for herself to be a quasi-redeemer or a co-redeemer: no. There is only one Redeemer and this title cannot be duplicated. She is merely disciple and Mother. And thus, it is as Mother we need to think of her, seek her and pray to her. She is the Mother. In the Mother Church. In the maternity of Our Lady we see the maternity of the Church who welcomes everyone, the good and the evil ones: everyone.[26]

Although some supporters of the proposed fifth dogma may see this as a setback, on May 13, 2023, in his message to Archbishop Gian Franco of the Sardinian Archdiocese of Sassari, using one of the Church's ancient titles, he invoked Mary as "Mediatrix of all graces," a title that affirms her role in the dispensation of grace.[27] Nevertheless, the good news is that the Second Vatican Council encouraged theologians to continue this conversation, contributing to the Church's understanding of Mary in the Church:

Wherefore this Holy Synod, in expounding the doctrine on the Church, in which the divine Redeemer works salvation, intends to describe with diligence both the role of the Blessed Virgin in the mystery of the Incarnate Word and the Mystical Body, and the duties of redeemed mankind toward the Mother of God, who is mother of Christ and mother of men, particularly of the faithful. *It does not, however, have it in mind to give a complete doctrine on Mary, nor does it wish to decide those questions which the work of theologians has not yet fully clarified.* Those opinions therefore may be lawfully retained which are propounded in Catholic schools concerning her, who occupies a place in the Church which is the highest after Christ and yet very close to us.[28]

Similarly, Pope Paul VI, writing before the completion of *Lumen Gentium*, in which the above paragraph is found, was aware that knowledge "of the true Catholic doctrine regarding the Blessed Virgin Mary will always be key to the exact understanding of Christ and of the Church" (*LG* 54).[29]

What Would a New Marian Dogma Mean for Women?

Early Christian writers referred to three elements used in the fall and in the redemption of humanity: a woman (Eve/Mary—New Eve/helpmate/associate), a man (Adam/Jesus—New Adam), and a tree (cross).[30] The symmetry in the reversal of the fall reflects the balance between the elements, reflecting the actions of the male and the female. Aidan Nichols writes, "That the New Adam should have a helpmate in the achieving of salvation who was a human person befits the structure of salvation and, if this is a female person we are talking about, enhances the symmetry of redemption in the inversion of fall."[31] Just as Eve is a helpmate for Adam (Gen 2:18), Mary is the "helpmate of the Redeemer,"[32] contributing to our redemption as a "true collaborator." Accordingly, a deeper analysis of the word "helper" or "helpmate" as it appears in Genesis 2:18 is needed to shed light on God's intended plan for men and women to be coresponsible in life and love. In 2004, the Congregation for the Doctrine of the Faith, in its commentary on the second creation account, included this impactful footnote in its document, *Letter to the Bishops of the Catholic Church on the Collaboration of Men and Women in the Church and in the World*:

> The Hebrew word *ezer*, which is translated as "helpmate," indicates the assistance which only a person can render to another. It carries no implication of inferiority or exploitation if we remember that God too is at times called *ezer* with regard to human beings (cf. Exod 18:4; Ps 10:14).[33]

Later in the document, the CDF affirms God's intended plan for humanity involves an affirmation of "equal dignity, physical, physiological, and ontological complementarity" (8). Moreover, the CDF refers to Paul's teaching on equality in Christ found in Galatians 3:28, commenting that equality does not imply a lack of distinction:

> The Apostle Paul does not say distinction between man and woman, which in other places is referred to the plan of God, has been erased. He means rather that in Christ the rivalry, enmity, and violence which disfigured the relationship between men and women can be overcome and have been overcome. (12)

Marian Approaches to Synodality

In other words, distinction is not to be used to oppress and silence, signaling the presence of evil and fear. Recall the prophecy found in Genesis 3:15, that there will be "enmity" between the serpent or evil one and the woman. Enmity or hostility toward "the woman" enters the picture after the fall. The evil one opposes and fears "the woman" because God chooses her to be a cocreator, relying on her cooperation to help bring about our salvation. This signals God's plan involves an affirmation of equality, coresponsibility and a shared humanity that participates in God's being. Hostility can be overcome when we do God's will. Mary, says Pope John Paul II, is our "sure hope" in this regard:

> Mary, Mother of the Incarnate Word, is placed at the very center of that enmity, that struggle which accompanies the history of humanity on earth and the history of salvation itself. In this central place, she who belongs to the "weak and poor of the Lord" bears in herself, like no other member of the human race, that "glory of grace" which the Father "has bestowed on us in his beloved Son," and this grace determines the extraordinary greatness and beauty of her whole being. Mary thus remains before God, and also before the whole of humanity, as the unchangeable and inviolable sign of God's election, spoken of in Paul's letter: "in Christ...he chose us... before the foundation of the world,...he destined us...to be his sons" (Eph 1:4, 5). This election is more powerful than any experience of evil and sin, than all that "enmity" which marks the history of man. In this history Mary remains a sign of sure hope.[34]

Not only is Mary Jesus's helper, but she is also our helper, showing us how we can overcome hostility and serve God, together with other men and women.

Mary

Using the biblical meaning of helper (*ezer*) or understanding women as "associates" or "helpmates" to clergy, may shed light on the role of women in the Church, men and women serving together, imaging God. Although not equal in significance, liturgical art reflects this complementarity with depictions of the Last Supper with Jesus at the center and depictions of Pentecost with Mary at the center. At the Last Supper, Jesus gave us his body, and at Pentecost we celebrate the extension of his body, with which Mary is closely identified as the model of the Church. Although by virtue of our baptism we are "formed in the likeness of Christ" (*LG* 7), identifying Mary as a coredeemer, as one working "with" Jesus makes it easier to create a pathway for women as "another Mary," whether this be as an instituted evangelist or in some other role such as a women's ministry leader. Just as Mary participates in Jesus's mission, one with him due to their shared humanity, we, too, participate in his mission, as an extension of his body, also her body—unity with distinction.

The ministry of women would make the collaboration between Jesus and Mary available in an old/new way with a new formal institutional expression. The old refers to Mary's position in the early Church with "certain women." The new refers to women representing some renewed attention, or a deepened understanding of Mary's role in salvation history. Without doubt, the issue of women in the Church has ontological, sociological, and ideological implications. The completion of our understanding of Mary's role in salvation history, however, could contribute to the development of a theology of women, thereby addressing the ontological concerns associated with the question of women and ministry.

In his apostolic letter *Ordinatio Sacerdotalis*, Pope John Paul II, repeating the instruction found in the Declaration *Inter Insigniores*,[35] continued to teach how the successors of the apostles and those who share in their ministry "carry on the Apostles' mission of representing Christ the Lord and the Redeemer."[36] Although all baptized people, male and female, "are formed in the likeness of Christ" (*LG* 7) making us "participants of the divine nature" (2 Pet 1:4), thereby equal in dignity, John Paul II emphasizes how Christ "choosing apostles only from among men" shows how priestly ordination "hands on the office entrusted by Christ to his Apostles."[37] Following his declaration associating the maleness of the apostles and the representation of Jesus, John Paul II says this about Mary:

> Furthermore, the fact that the Blessed Virgin Mary, Mother of God and Mother of the Church, received neither the mission proper to the Apostles nor the ministerial priesthood clearly shows that the non-admission of women to priestly ordination cannot mean that women are of lesser dignity, nor can it be construed as discrimination against them. Rather, it is to be seen as the faithful observance of a plan to be ascribed to the wisdom of the Lord of the universe.
>
> The presence and the role of women in the life and mission of the Church, although not linked to the ministerial priesthood, *remain absolutely necessary and irreplaceable*.[38]

Hence, if Mary did not receive the "mission proper to the Apostles" meaning "the Twelve," did her anointing signal another mission? Is there a mission proper to Mary and "certain women?" Was she, the Queen of the Apostles, set apart for another complementary type of apostolic ministry? If the "presence and the role of women in the life and mission of the Church" is not linked to the ministerial priesthood, how can we show that their role is "absolutely necessary and irreplaceable"? An earlier document on the question of women and ordination suggests "the Church desires that Christian women should

Mary

become *fully aware* of the greatness of their mission: today their role is of capital importance both for the renewal and humanization of society and for the *rediscovery by believers of the true face of the Church*."[39] It's been roughly forty-seven years since this statement was made. How many women know they are called to be the "true face of the Church"? If Mary "mirrors" the Church, the body of Christ, do women see themselves reflected in the Church?

Apart from affirming the very important role of women in family life, the contributions of consecrated women, and the contributions of women in the various sectors that serve the wider community, does Mary's role in salvation history inform the development of a formal institutional expression of the Marian dimension in the Church? The successors of the apostles, the bishops, represent a formal institutional expression of their anointing. It follows that Mary, the Queen of the Apostles, should inspire some discernment of a complementary and formal expression of her presence in the Church.

With their shared humanity, men and women image God (Gen 1:27); complementarity in ministry, or shared ministry, would reflect balance and harmony—men and women walking and standing with the people of God, ministering to their needs, and listening to their stories. This harkens back to the Council of Jerusalem in Acts 15, where "the Twelve" invite apostles of another class, or category, meaning they were not part of the original Twelve, namely, Paul and Barnabas, to dialogue and discern the future of Christianity. Although the distinction between the apostolic ministry of the twelve and their successors and women remains mainly rooted in the laying on of hands received by the men, signaling a unique calling, the Church has referred to women with special honorary titles; for example, Mary as the Queen of the Apostles, Mary Magdalene, St. Photine, and St. Faustina.[40] Moreover, the postconciliar document on women and evangelization referred to early biblical

Marian Approaches to Synodality

women as "apostles," itinerant preachers who shared the good news of Jesus.[41]

To go forward with this conversation, the Church requires men and women, clergy, consecrated, and nonconsecrated laypeople to enter dialogue, praying, discerning, and welcoming the power of the Holy Spirit to complete our understanding of Mary's role in our redemption and the role of women in the Church. Mary and "certain women" prayed together with the eleven apostles in the upper room.[42] What would it look like to have women, in a more formal role, accompanying the magisterium in prayer and discernment? Is the Holy Spirit calling us to discern a formal institutional expression of another Mary, revealing the deeper meaning of Church, walking with the people of God as Mother and Teacher? Is the Synod on Synodality providing this opportunity? What is God's will regarding a complete doctrine of Mary and the role of women in the Church? Cardinal Ratzinger in *The Ratzinger Report* states:

> If the place occupied by Mary has been essential to the equilibrium of the faith, today it is urgent, as in few other epochs of the Church, to rediscover that place. It is necessary to go back to Mary if we want to return to that "truth about Jesus Christ."[43]

We can only discern this outcome when we approach the discernment like Mary, with humility, patience, obedience, and receptivity to the promptings of the Holy Spirit. Let us not be afraid to approach the topic with sincerity, asking the Holy Spirit for clarity in the manner of Mary. The Synod on Synodality has provided an opportunity for discernment and growth. May our Marian "yes" to do God's will, inspired by the Holy Spirit, grant us *wisdom* to know and recognize God's "go" when it comes to knowing how to proceed:

Mary

For she is a breath of the power of God, and a pure emanation of the glory of the Almighty....For she is a reflection of eternal light, a spotless *mirror* of the working of God, and an *image* of his goodness....I loved her and sought her from my youth; I desired to take her for my *bride*, and became enamored with her beauty. For she is an initiate in the knowledge of God, and an *associate* in his works (Wis 7:25–26; 8:1, 4).[44]

Notes

Chapter 1

1. This type of fear, an emotional response to an imagined or real threat, is to be distinguished from the gift of the Spirit known as the "fear of the Lord." See *CCC* 1831. "Fear of the Lord" speaks of awe. Pope Francis, in a general audience on June 11, 2014, had this to say about "fear of the Lord": "[Fear of the Lord] does not mean being afraid of God: we know well that God is Father, that he loves us and wants our salvation, and he always forgives, always; thus, there is no reason to be scared of him! Fear of the Lord, instead, is the gift of the Holy Spirit through whom we are reminded of how small we are before God and of his love and that our good lies in humble, respectful and trusting self-abandonment into his hands. This is fear of the Lord: abandonment in the goodness of our Father who loves us so much." https://www.vatican.va/content/francesco/en/audiences/2014/documents/papa-francesco_20140611_udienza-generale.html.

2. See *CCC* 777. *Church* means convocation or assembly of believers.

3. See the research of Gabor Maté, *When the Body Says No* (Random House: Toronto, 2003) and *The Myth of Normal: Trauma, Illness and Healing in a Toxic Culture* (Toronto: Penguin Random House, 2022). See also Bessel Van der Kolk, *The Body Keeps the Score: Brain, Mind, and Body in the Healing of Trauma* (Penguin Books: New York, 2015). Love forms the child and informs their sense of identity.

Marian Approaches to Synodality

4. For example, models that are found in scripture, and affirmed in Church teaching, namely, among others, Church as the people of God (1 Pet 2:9–12), *LG* 12; Church as Body of Christ (1 Cor 12:27) *LG* 7; Church as Temple of the Holy Spirit (2 Cor 6:16), *LG* 17. For more on models of the Church, see Cardinal Avery Dulles, *Models of the Church* (Image Press, Lloydminster, 1991).

5. Pope John XXIII referred to the Church as mother and teacher in his encyclical, *Mater et Magistra* [Christianity and Social Progress] (1961), 1.

6. See Julie Hasson and Missy Lenard, *Unmapped Potential: An Educator's Guide to Lasting Change* (San Diego: Dave Burgess Publishing, 2017).

7. See *LG* 5: "The Church…is also called our mother." In their final document of the Asian Continental Assembly, the Asian Bishops' Conference refers to the Church as a "good Mother." See Federation of Asian Bishops' Conferences, *Final Document of the Asian Continental Assembly on Synodality*, March 16, 2023, 58 and 99, https://fabc.org/wp-content/uploads/2023/03/ACAS-Final-Document-16-Mar-2023.pdf.

8. I refer to the external curriculum and the internal curriculum in my book, *Experts in Humanity: A Journey of Self-Discovery and Healing* (Novalis: Toronto, 2016). In this book, I focus on the internal curriculum using a multidisciplinary approach to human formation.

9. Pope Francis, general audience, September 13, 2023, https://www.vatican.va/content/francesco/en/audiences/2023/documents/20230913-udienza-generale.html.

10. Commission on Spirituality Sub-group, Spirituality for Synodality, *Towards a Spirituality for Synodality* 52, https://www.usccb.org/resources/towards-spirituality-synodality. See also *CCC* 2030. "It is in the Church, in communion with all the baptized, that the Christian fulfills his vocation. From the Church he receives the Word of God containing the teachings of 'the law of Christ.' From the Church he receives the grace of the sacraments that sustains him on the 'way.' From the Church he learns the example of holiness and recognizes its model and source in the all-holy virgin Mary; he discerns it in the authentic witness of those who live it; he discovers it in the spiritual tradition and long history of the saints who have gone before him and

Notes

whom the liturgy celebrates in the rhythms of the sanctoral cycle," emphasis mine.

11. Commission on Spirituality Sub-group, *Towards a Spirituality for Synodality*, 45.

12. For more on Church as communion of believers, see CDF, "Letter to Bishops of the Catholic Church on Some Aspects of Church Understood as Communion," https://www.vatican.va/roman_curia/congregations/cfaith/documents/rc_con_cfaith_doc_28051992_communionis-notio_en.html.

13. Pope Francis, "Pope Francis' Speech in Fatima," August 4, 2023, https://www.lisboa2023.org/en/article/pope-francis-speech-in-fatima.

14. See Preparatory Document, *For a Synodal Church: Communion, Participation, and Mission*, September 7, 2021, 10, https://www.synod.va/en/news/the-preparatory-document.html.

15. Commission on Spirituality Sub-group, *Towards a Spirituality for Synodality*, 45.

16. General Secretariat of the Synod, "With Mary towards the Synodal Assembly," March 15, 2023, https://www.synod.va/en/news/with-mary-towards-the-synodal-assembly.html.

17. Pope Paul VI declared Mary "Mother of the Church" in his address at the conclusion of the third session of the Second Vatican Council. See "The Council for the Promulgation of the Constitution of the Church," November 21, 1964. In 2018, Pope Francis decreed that "the Memorial of the Blessed Virgin Mary, Mother of the Church, should be celebrated on the Monday after Pentecost."

18. For more on the process of synodality, see Moira McQueen, *Walking Together: A Primer on the New Synodality* (Novalis: Toronto, 2022).

19. Pope Francis, homily, Solemnity of St. Peter and St. Paul, June 29, 2022, https://www.vatican.va/content/francesco/en/homilies/2022/documents/20220629-omelia-pallio.html.

20. Pope Francis, Address for the Ceremony Commemorating the Fiftieth Anniversary of the Institution of the Synod of Bishops, October 17, 2015.

21. *Vademecum* [Handbook for the Synod on Synodality] September 2021, 1.1, https://www.synod.va/content/dam/synod/document/common/vademecum/Vademecum-EN-A4.pdf.

Marian Approaches to Synodality

22. See ITC, *Synodality in the Life and Mission of the Church*, 2017, https://www.vatican.va/roman_curia/congregations/cfaith/cti_documents/rc_cti_20180302_sinodalita_en.html.

23. Pope Paul VI, *Apostolica Sollicitudo* [Establishing the Synod of Bishops for the Universal Church] September 15, 1965, https://www.vatican.va/content/paul-vi/en/motu_proprio/documents/hf_p-vi_motu-proprio_19650915_apostolica-sollicitudo.html.

24. Paul VI, *Establishing the Synod of Bishops*.

25. Paul VI, *Establishing the Synod of Bishops*.

26. For example, the Synod on Young People, the Fifteenth Ordinary General Assembly of the Synod of Bishops, October 3–28, 2018. An Ordinary General Assembly occurs when "the matters under discussion, pertain to the good of the universal Church (*EC* 1.1).

27. For example, Pope Francis announced in 2013 that an Extraordinary General Assembly of the Synod of Bishops on topics related to the family and evangelization would take place in October of 2014. The Extraordinary General Assembly was followed by an Ordinary General Assembly of the Synod of Bishops in October of 2015, on the same topics. Extraordinary General Assemblies occur when "the matters under discussion, pertaining to the good of the universal Church, require urgent consideration" (*EC* 1.2).

28. An example of a Special Session is the Special Assembly of the Synod of Bishops for the Pan-Amazon Region, October 6–27, 2019. See http://secretariat.synod.va/content/sinodoamazonico/en/documents/final-document-of-the-amazon-synod.html. Special Assemblies occur when "matters are discussed which pertain principally to one or more particular geographic areas" (*EC* 1.3).

29. See Pope Francis, *Episcopalis Communio*, September 15, 2018, n. 1.1-1.3, https://www.vatican.va/content/francesco/en/apost_constitutions/documents/papa-francesco_costituzione-ap_20180915_episcopalis-communio.html.

30. For more details on the composition of membership, see Pope Paul VI, Establishing the Synod of Bishops.

31. For an incomplete list, see https://www.vatican.va/news_services/press/documentazione/documents/sinodo_indice_en.html.

Notes

32. See Lorenzo Cardinal Baldisseri, Synod General Secretary, *Communiqué*, February 17, 2016, https://press.vatican.va/content/salastampa/en/bollettino/pubblico/2017/11/21/171121e.html.
33. ITC, *Synodality in the Life and Mission of the Church*, 3.
34. ITC, *Synodality in the Life and Mission of the Church*, 3, 4.
35. ITC, *Synodality in the Life and Mission of the Church*, 3.
36. See ITC, *Synodality in the Life and Mission of the Church*, 40.
37. Moira McQueen, *Walking Together: A Primer on the New Synodality* (Toronto: Novalis, 2022), Introduction, 6. Moira McQueen explains the word *council* derives from Latin (*con*) "together with," while *synod* derives from Greek (*syn*) "way."
38. McQueen, *Walking Together*, 7.
39. Pope Francis, Address during the Ceremony Commemorating the Fiftieth Anniversary of the Institution of the Synod of Bishops, October 17, 2015, 6. The Synod on the Family provided the context for the address. https://www.vatican.va/content/francesco/en/speeches/2015/october/documents/papa-francesco_20151017_50-anniversario-sinodo.html.
40. Pope Francis, Ceremony Commemorating the Fiftieth Anniversary, 7.
41. ITC, *Synodality in the Life and Mission of the Church*, 67.
42. ITC, *Synodality in the Life and Mission of the Church*, 103.
43. On March 10, 2023, in an interview with *La Nación*, Pope Francis told journalist Elisabetta Pique that although invited observers cannot vote, female representatives will vote during the Synod on Synodality. For a summary of the interview, visit https://www.vaticannews.va/en/pope/news/2023-03/pope-francis-i-dream-of-a-more-pastoral-more-open-church.html. Moira McQueen addressed this topic during the writing of the ITC document on synodality. For more background, see McQueen, *Walking Together*, 58.
44. See Chris Herlinger, "Sr. Nathalie Becquart: 'Yes, Yes, I Will Be Voting at the Synod on Synodality,'" March 31, 2023, https://www.globalsistersreport.org/news/sr-nathalie-becquart-yes-yes-i-will-be-voting-synod-synodality.
45. See Christopher White, "Pope Francis Expands Participation in Synod to Lay Members, Granting Right to Vote," *National Catholic Reporter*, April 26, 2023, https://www.ncronline.org/vatican/vatican

-news/pope-francis-expands-participation-synod-lay-members-granting-right-vote#:~:text=Pope%20Francis%20on%20April%2026,Catholic%20Church's%20primary%20consultative%20body.

46. For more background on the first nonordained representative vote, see Colleen Dulle, "Why Can't Women Vote at the Synod on Young People?" October 1, 2018, https://www.americamagazine.org/faith/2018/10/10/why-cant-women-vote-synod-young-people.

47. See Christopher Lamb, "Synod and Laudate Deum. Updates from Rome," The Tablet, October 4, 2023, https://www.thetablet.co.uk/news/17705/synod-and-laudate-deum-updates-from-rome.

48. Preparatory Document, 10.

49. *Vademecum*, 5.3, cf. Preparatory Document, 26.

50. ITC, *Sensus Fidei*, 2014, chapters 1 and 2, https://www.vatican.va/roman_curia/congregations/cfaith/cti_documents/rc_cti_20140610_butler-sensus-fidei_en.html.

51. Jos Moons, "A Comprehensive Introduction to Synodality: Reconfiguring Ecclesiology and Ecclesial Practice," in *Annals of Theology* 69, no.2 (2022), 73–93.

52. For more details regarding the process involved in the four phases, visit https://www.synod.va/en/resources.html.

53. Pope Francis, video message, May 26, 2022, https://www.vatican.va/content/francesco/en/events/event.dir.html/content/vaticanevents/en/2022/5/26/videomessaggio-plenaria-pcal.html.

54. Michael Sean Winters, "How Will a Synodal Church Embody the Virtue of Obedience?" *National Catholic Reporter*, April 10, 2023.

55. Winters, "How Will a Synodal Church Embody the Virtue of Obedience?"

56. ITC, "Synodality in the Life and Mission of the Church," 46.

57. ITC, "Synodality in the Life and Mission of the Church," 50.

58. Commission on Spirituality Sub-Group, *Towards a Spirituality for Synodality*, 11. See also Jos Moons, "The Holy Spirit as the Protagonist of the Synod: Pope Francis's Creative Reception of the Second Vatican Council," *Theological Studies* 84, no. 1 (2023): 61–78.

59. See ITC, *Synodality in the Life and Mission of the Church*, 108.

60. ITC, *Synodality in the Life and Mission of the Church*, 47.

61. See Preparatory Document, 15. Cf. *LG*, 48.

Notes

62. See Preparatory Document, 15. Cf. *LG*, 1. See also *Towards a Spirituality for Synodality*, 13. Communion is seen as "a Trinitarian reality."

63. A careful study of scripture reveals that both the verb *to save* and the noun *salvation* are connected to restoration/healing (Luke 8:48), forgiveness (Luke 1:77), deliverance from harm and evil (Matt 8:23–27), conversion/doing God's will (Luke 19:1–10), becoming God's adopted sons and daughters (Rom 11:14), eternal life with God (1 Cor 3:15), and the beatific vision (1 Cor 13:12).

64. See 1 Tim 2:4; also Josephine Lombardi, *What Are They Saying about the Universal Salvific Will of God?* (Paulist Press: Mahwah, New Jersey, 2008).

65. *EC* 1.

66. See Moons, "A Comprehensive Introduction to Synodality," 74.

67. Commission on Spirituality Sub-group, *Towards a Spirituality for Synodality*, 45.

Chapter 2

1. ITC, *Synodality in the Life and Mission of the Church*, 2018, 12, emphasis mine.

2. Commission on Spirituality Sub-group, Spirituality for Synodality, *Towards a Spirituality for Synodality*, 47–48. Visit https://www.usccb.org/resources/towards-spirituality-synodality.

3. See Gary Devery, "Marian and Petrine Dimensions of the Church" April 4, 2003, www.clerus.org.

4. See *CCC* 1996–1997.

5. Cardinal Joseph Ratzinger, *Mary, the Church at Its Source* (San Francisco: Ignatius Press, 2005), 68.

6. See Joseph A. Fisher, *A Catechetical Dictionary for the Catechism of the Catholic Church* (New Bedford: Academy of the Immaculate, 2016), 587. Fisher defines type as "anything that represents, foreshadows, or symbolizes something else."

7. CDF, "Letter to the Bishops of the Catholic Church on Some Aspects of the Church Understood as Communion," n. 19, May 28,

Marian Approaches to Synodality

1992, https://www.vatican.va/roman_curia/congregations/cfaith/doc uments/rc_con_cfaith_doc_28051992_communionis-notio_en.html.

8. See Pope Paul VI, apostolic exhortation *Marialus Cultus* [For the Right Ordering and Development of Devotion to the Blessed Virgin Mary], 1974, 16–23, https://www.vatican.va/content/paul-vi/en/apost_exhortations/documents/hf_p-vi_exh_19740202_marialis-cultus.html.

9. CDF, "Letter to the Bishops of the Catholic Church on the Collaboration of Men and Women in the Church and in the World," May 31, 2004, 15, https://www.vatican.va/roman_curia/congregations/cfaith/documents/rc_con_cfaith_doc_20040731_collaboration_en.html.

10. CDF, "On the Collaboration of Men and Women in the Church and in the World," 16.

11. CDF, "On the Collaboration of Men and Women in the Church and in the World," 16.

12. See Pope John Paul II, general audience, "The Marian and Petrine Principles," December 22, 1997, www.vatican.va.

13. Devery, "Marian and Petrine Dimensions of the Church."

14. John Paul II, general audience, "The Marian and Petrine Dimension."

15. The image of Church as bride has inspired more thought on the feminine dimension of the Church. See *CCC*, 796. More on this in the next chapter.

16. Pope Francis, in-flight press conference from Sweden to Rome, November 1, 2016, https://www.vatican.va/content/francesco/en/speeches/2016/november/documents/papa-francesco_20161101_svezia-conferenza-stampa.html.

17. Cardinal Joseph Ratzinger, "Don't Forget Mary" (1984), Excerpt from Cardinal Joseph Ratzinger and Vittorio Messori, *The Ratzinger Report: An Exclusive Interview on the State of the Church* (San Francisco: Ignatius Press, 1985), 108.

18. Cardinal Joseph Ratzinger, *Mary, the Church at Its Source* (San Francisco: Ignatius Press, 2005), 27.

19. *Ecclesio*-typical Mariology emphasizes Mary as figure, image, or type of the Church, cf. *LG*, 68.

20. See Aidan Nichols, *There Is No Rose* (Fortress Press, 2015), 140–47. Nichols explores the tension between Christo-typical Mari-

ology, one that emphasizes Mary's divine motherhood, a more Christ-centered approach, and *Ecclesio*-typical Mariology, or a Church-centered approach that emphasizes Mary as "type of the Church."

21. Ratzinger, "Don't Forget Mary," 109.

22. See Hans Urs von Balthasar, "Women Priests? A Marian Church in a Fatherless and Motherless Culture," *Communio* 22.1, 1995: 164–70.

23. John Paul II, *Mulieris Dignitatem*, 27.

24. Sara Marie Kowal, "The Identification of the Blessed Virgin Mary: Unconditional Service to the Petrine Principle," www.piercedhearts.org.

25. John Paul II, *Mulieris Dignitatem*, 27.

26. Pope Francis, Letter to Cardinal Marc Ouellet, President of the Pontifical Commission for Latin America, March 19, 2016. English translation in *L'Osservatore Romano*, April 29, 2016, English edition, 4–5. For a further contemporary reflection on clericalism, see George B. Wilson, *Clericalism: The Death of Priesthood* (Collegeville, MN: Liturgical Press, 2008).

27. See John Paul II, *Mulieris Dignitatem*, 27.

28. See Margaret Harper McCarthy, "The Feminine Genius and Women's Contributions in Society and the Church," in Mary Rice Hasson, ed., *Promise and Challenge: Catholic Women Reflect on Feminism, Complementarity, and the Church* (Huntington, IN: Our Sunday Visitor, 2015), 125.

29. See "Priesthood in the 21st Century: Vatican Encourages Reflection on Its Challenges," February 26, 2023, https://www.romereports.com/en/2023/02/26/priesthood-in-the-21st-century-vatican-encourages-reflection-on-its-challenges/.

30. See di Marinella Perroni, "*Il Duplice Principio*," in *L'Osservatore Romano* (December 3, 2022), https://www.osservatoreromano.va/it/news/2022-12/dcm-011/il-duplice-principio.html.

31. Pope John Paul II, Address to the Cardinals and Prelates of the Roman Curia, *L'Osservatore Romano* (December 23, 1987).

32. John Paul II, Address to the Cardinals and Prelates of the Roman Curia.

33. See Monica Migliorino Miller, *The Authority of Women in the Catholic Church* (Steubenville, OH: Emmaus Road, 2015), 151.

34. See the Federation of Asian Bishops' Conferences, "Final Document of the Asian Continental Assembly on Synodality," March 16, 2023, 58 and 99, https://fabc.org/wp-content/uploads/2023/03/ACAS-Final-Document-16-Mar-2023.pdf.

35. Pope Paul VI, address, November 21, 1964, quoted in John Paul II, *Redemptoris Mater*, 47.

36. Some Catholics have lamented their lack of understanding of the Marian dimension. This criticism came up in an article including readers' input in *America* magazine, December 21, 2022, in response to an earlier interview with Pope Francis. Rachel Lu, a reader, contributed the following feedback, "I confess that I also do not entirely understand when he (Pope Francis) talks about the Marian principle."

37. Pope Francis, *The Name of God Is Mercy*, 6.

38. See Josephine Lombardi, "Mercy and Beyond: Pope Francis' Marian 'Program of Life.'" *Ecce Mater Tua* 2 (2019): 3–24, https://eccematertua.com/sites/ecce/files/uploads/documents/mercy_and_beyond_-_pope_francis_marian_program_of_life.pdf.

39. Pope Francis, *"Misericordiae Vultus:* Bull of Indication for the Extraordinary Jubilee of Mercy," *Origins* 44, no. 46 (2015): 745–54, §13.

40. Lombardi, "Mercy and Beyond," 5.

41. Massimo Faggioli, "From Collegiality to Synodality: Promise and Limits of Francis's 'Listening Primacy.'" *Irish Theological Quarterly* 85, no. 4 (2020): 366.

42. Lombardi, "Mercy and Beyond," 3.

43. The Book of Wisdom captures this delicate dynamic between mercy and justice; see 11:9–14. See also Psalms 90–106.

44. Chapter 4 will explore this insight in greater detail.

45. Lombardi, "Mercy and Beyond," 9.

46. See Josephine Lombardi, *Experts in Humanity: A Journey of Self-Discovery and Healing* (Toronto: Novalis, 2016).

47. See Julian of Norwich, "The Fourteenth Showing," in *The Revelation of Divine Love in Sixteen Showings Made to Dame Julian of Norwich*, trans. M. L. del Mastro (Liguori, MO: Ligouri Press, 1994), 167–68.

48. Julian of Norwich, "The Fourteenth Showing," 169.

Notes

49. Julian of Norwich, "The Fourteenth Showing," 167.

50. Julian of Norwich, "The Fourteenth Showing," 168.

51. Julian of Norwich, "The First Showing," in *The Revelation of Divine Love in Sixteen Showings Made to Dame Julian of Norwich*, trans. M. L. del Mastro (Liguori, MO: Ligouri Press, 1994), 71.

52. Kevin Clarke, "The Mother of Fair Love: The Beauty of the Ever-Virgin for the Vocations of Christian Life," *Marian Studies* 66, article 8 (2015): 188, https://ecommons.udayton.edu/marian_studies/vol66/iss1/8.

53. Adrienne von Speyr, *Mary in the Redemption* (San Francisco: Ignatius Press, 1979), 20.

54. Von Speyr, *Mary in the Redemption*, 32.

55. An expression used by early Christian writers. See Justin Martyr, *Dialogue with Trypho*, ch. 100, PG 6, 709–12; Irenaeus of Lyon, *Adversus Haereses*, III, ch. 22, 4, PG 7, 959. Just as St. Paul refers to Jesus as the New Adam (1 Cor 15:22, 45), Mary is considered the New Eve.

56. For more on Mary as the First Lady, see my film, "The First Lady and Her Successors," found at www.josephinelombardi.com.

57. Pope Benedict XVI, homily, "Solemnity of the Immaculate Conception of the Blessed Virgin Mary," December 8, 2005, https://www.vatican.va/content/benedict-xvi/en/homilies/2005/documents/hf_ben-xvi_hom_20051208_anniv-vat-council.html, emphasis mine.

58. While there are many references to *ecclesio*-typical and *Christo*-typical approaches to Mariology, I refer to the study of Mary and the Holy Spirit as a *pneuma*-typical approach.

59. Benedict XVI, homily, "Solemnity of the Immaculate Conception."

60. See John Paul II, general audience, May 28, 1997, 3, https://www.vaticava/content/john-paul-ii/en/audiences/1997/documents/hf_jp-ii_aud_28051997.html.

61. The dogma of the Immaculate Conception of Mary completes our understanding regarding this mystery. The dogma was solemnly defined and declared on December 8, 1854. Pope Pius IX pronounced and solemnly sanctioned "that the doctrine, which holds that the Most Blessed Virgin Mary at the first moment of her conception was, by singular grace and privilege of the Omnipotent God, in

virtue of the merits of Jesus Christ, Savior of the Human race, preserved from all stains of original sin, is revealed by God, and therefore to be firmly and resolutely believed by all the faithful." Dogmatic bull *Ineffabilis Deus*, December 8, 1854.

62. Pope Pius IX, *Ineffabilis Deus*, 1854, https://www.papalencyclicals.net/pius09/p9ineff.htm.

63. *CCC* 493.

64. See Paul VI, *Marialus Cultus*, 26.

65. See 1 Cor 6:19: "Or do you not know your body is a temple of the Holy Spirit within you, which you have from God, and that you are not your own."

66. Cf. Gen 1:26ff; 5:1–3; 9:6.

67. CDF, Letter to the Bishops of the Catholic Church on Men and Women in the Church and in the World, 17.

68. See *CCC* 356–357.

69. See *CCC* 364 regarding the dignity of the body: "The human body shares in the dignity of 'the image of God': it is a human body precisely because it is animated by a spiritual soul, and it is the whole human person that is intended to become, in the body of Christ, a temple of the spirit." Similarly, the ITC, in its biblical reflection on the image of God, reminds us that the whole of the person "is seen as created in the image of God. See the ITC, *Communion and Stewardship: Human Persons Created in the Image of God*, 2002, 9, https://www.vatican.va/roman_curia/congregations/cfaith/cti_documents/rc_con_cfaith_doc_20040723_communion-stewardship_en.html.

70. Sadly, however, early abuse and trauma, prenatally and postnatally, can prevent the flourishing of these capacities. See Lombardi, *Experts in Humanity*.

71. Lombardi, *Experts in Humanity*.

72. Preparatory Document. *For a Synodal Church: Communion, Participation, and Mission*, September 7, 2021, 2, https://www.synod.va/en/news/the-preparatory-document.html.

73. ITC, *Synodality in the Life and Mission of the Church*, 138.

74. ITC, *Synodality in the Life and Mission of the Church*, 109.

75. This brief reflection on Maximus the Confessor's *The Life of the Virgin* is a slightly developed version of my article "*In Persona Mariae*: Another Mary for Another Christ—Women as Marian Suc-

cessors in Seminary Formation," in *For the Love of the Church: A Festschrift on the Interests and Accomplishments of His Eminence Thomas Cardinal Collins*, ed. Peter Lovrick (Toronto: Novalis, 2022), 315–43. Used with permission. In this article I use Maximus the Confessor's *The Life of the Virgin*, translated by Stephen J. Shoemaker, as the framework for the discussion. Although this *Life of the Virgin* has been attributed to Maximus the Confessor, scholars such as Maximas Constans and Christos Simelides, argue that John Geometres (ca. 935–1000 CE) is the true author of the manuscript. The Middle Byzantine Library of Marian Hagiography includes versions of the *Life of the Virgin* prepared by Epiphanios of Kallistros, Ps.-Maximus, Symeon Metaphastes, and John Geometres. The research of Constans and Simelides can be found in "Antoine Wenger and John Geometre's Life of the Virgin," in *The Reception of the Virgin in Byzantium: Marian Texts and Images*, ed. Thomas Arentzen and Mary B. Cunningham (New York: Cambridge University Press, 2019), 60.

76. Maximus the Confessor, *The Life of the Virgin*, trans. Stephen J. Shoemaker (New Haven, CT: Yale University Press, 2012), 1.

77. Maximus the Confessor, *Life of the Virgin*, 121.

78. Maximus the Confessor, *Life of the Virgin*, 124.

79. Maximus the Confessor, *Life of the Virgin*, 126.

80. See Ally Kateusz, *Mary and Early Christian Women: Hidden Leadership* (Cham, Switzerland: Palgrave/Macmillan, 2019).

81. Pope John Paul II, general audience, May 28, 1997, 5, https://www.vatican.va/content/john-paul-ii/en/audiences/1997/documents/hf_jp-ii_aud_28051997.html.

82. North American Synod Team, *North American Final Document for the Continental Stage of the 2021–2024 Synod*, April 12, 2023, 55, https://www.usccb.org/resources/North%20American%20Final%20Document%20-%20English.pdf.

83. Commentary on scriptural texts affirming Mary's intimacy with the Holy Spirit will accompany subsequent chapters.

84. Maximus the Confessor, *Life of the Virgin*, 124.

85. This insight will be explored in chapters 3 and 6.

86. Maximus the Confessor, *Life of the Virgin*, 102. Elsewhere, Maximus refers to "worthy myrrh-bearing women" who coministered with the apostles, naming them "co-apostles." See p. 123, emphasis

Marian Approaches to Synodality

mine. I produced, directed, and wrote a documentary titled *The First Lady and Her Successors*. Visit josephinelombardi.com.

87. See Gal 1:1; 1 Cor 1:1; 1 Tim 2:7; and Acts 26:12–18.

88. In the New Testament, we not only hear about Paul, but the following are referred to as apostles: Barnabas, James, Apollos, Epaphroditus, Andonius, Junias, Silas, and Timothy. In Sacred Tradition, the following women have been referred to as apostles: Mary Magdalene, St. Photine or the Woman at the Well, and St. Faustina, declared "Apostle of Divine Mercy."

89. Acts 13:3 acknowledges St. Paul receiving the laying on of hands and Acts 19:1–6, 1 Tim 4:14 and 2 Tim 1:6 document St. Paul laying hands on others, including Timothy. See also *CCC* 1590.

90. Fr. Joseph Chandrakanthan, "Water and Fire: The Person of the Holy Spirit in Christian Life," presentation, Lay Formation Days, St. Augustine's Seminary, Scarborough, Ontario, Canada, November 21, 2020.

91. Pope John Paul II writes, "Mary's maternal mediation does not obscure the unique and perfect mediation of Christ. Indeed, after calling Mary 'Mediatrix,' the Council is careful to explain that this 'neither takes away anything from nor adds anything to the dignity and efficacy of Christ the one Mediator' (*LG* 62). And on this subject, it quotes 1Tim 2:5–6: "For there is one God and there is one mediator between God and men, the man Christ Jesus, who gave himself as a ransom for all." See John Paul II, general audience, October 1, 1997, 3, https://www.vatican.va/content/john-paul-ii/en/audiences/1997/documents/hf_jp-ii_aud_01101997.html.

92. Maximillian Kolbe, *The Writings of Maximillian Kolbe*, trans. Cristoforo Zambelli (Rome: Militia of Mary Immaculate, 1997), 311, 428.

93. See James McCurry, "The Mariology of Maximilian Kolbe, *Marian Studies* 36, no. 12 (1985): 92. McCurry writes: "It is important to note immediately that Kolbe qualifies his attribution of the word 'incarnation' here by the phrase 'in a certain sense.' Elsewhere he speaks of the Holy Spirit as '*quasi-incarnatus*.'"

94. On May 26, 2002, Pope Francis, in a video message for the Plenary Assembly of the Pontifical Commission for Latin America, referred to synodality as being pneumatological and eucharistic.

Notes

95. Monsignor Arthur Burton Calkins, in his article "Our Lady's Presence in the Mass in the Teaching of Pope John Paul II," summarizes the thought of John Paul II on the bodily connection between Mary and Jesus this way, "The body and blood of Christ had its only human source in the body and blood of Mary: the flesh of Christ in the Eucharist is sacramentally the flesh assumed from the Virgin Mary. The Eucharist, then, while commemorating the passion and resurrection, is also in continuity with the incarnation and thus evokes Mary's presence." *Ecce Mater Tua* 2 (2019): 45–69, https://eccematertua.com/sites/ecce/files/uploads/documents/our_ladys_presence_in_the_mass_in_the_teaching_of_pope_john_paul_ii.pdf. Moreover, the world of science offers some insight into this mystery. The process of microchimerism refers to the transfer of some cells from the body of the fetus to the mother's body and the transfer of some cells from the mother's body to the body of the fetus. Visit www.microchimerism.org.

96. Also, the resurrection of Jesus, the firstfruits (1 Cor 15:20), made it possible for Mary to experience her bodily assumption into heaven.

97. See Pope John Paul II, encyclical letter *Redemptoris Mater*, 1987, 18.

98. Maximus the Confessor, *Life of the Virgin*, 30.

99. See 1 Pet 4:13: "But rejoice insofar as you are sharing Christ's sufferings, so that you may also be glad and shout for joy when his glory is revealed." See also Phil 3:8, 10–11.

100. See John Paul II, apostolic letter *Salvifici Doloris*, February 11, 1984.

101. Pope Benedict XVI, apostolic exhortation *Sacramentum Caritatis*, February 22, 2007, 33.

102. Magisterial teaching explains how the two expressions differ. Members of the common priesthood live out their priesthood "by the unfolding of baptismal grace" whereas members of the ministerial priesthood build up and teach members of the Church by and through their own sacrament, Holy Orders. See *CCC* 1547.

103. John Paul II, *Mulieris Dignitatem*, 27. Cf. *LG* 10 on the teaching on the baptismal priesthood. The bold emphasis is mine.

104. See Anne L. Clark, "The Priesthood of the Virgin Mary: Gender Trouble in the Twelfth Century," *Journal of Feminist Studies in Religion* 18, no. 1 (Spring 2002): 5–24. Clark highlights the contributions of Hildegard von Bingen and Elisabeth Shönau in the twelfth century.

105. See René Laurentin, *Marie, l'Eglise et la Sacerdoce* (Paris: Nouvelles Editions Latines, 1952). See also Emile Neubert, *Marie et Notre Sacerdoce* (Paris: Editions Spes, 1954).

106. See 1 Tim 2:5.

107. For more details on this topic, see John M. Samaha, "Mary's Sacerdotal Role" in *Homiletic & Pastoral Review* (December 1999): 10–17.

108. Nathan O'Halloran, "The Priesthood of Mary," https://whosoeverdesires.wordpress.com/2011/09/19/the-priesthood-of-mary/. For more on early images of Mary in priestly vestments, see Ally Kateusz, *Mary and Early Christian Women*, especially chapter 4.

109. University of Dayton, "All about Mary," https://udayton.edu/imri/mary/p/priesthood-and-mary.php. See *AAS* 40, 1909, 109.

110. See Laurentin, *Marie, l'Eglise et la Sacerdoce*, 509–38. See also *LG* 60.

111. See Clark, "The Priesthood of the Virgin Mary," 5–24. Anne L. Clark documents the treatment of the title "Mary, Virgin Priest" in the thought and writings of Hildegard von Bingen and her younger contemporary Elisabeth of Shönau.

112. Maximus the Confessor, *Life of the Virgin*, 124.

113. John Paul II, *Redemptoris Mater*, 44.

114. John Paul II, Address to Polish Pilgrims before Mass, August 25, 2001, emphasis mine, https://www.vatican.va/content/john-paul-ii/en/speeches/2001/august/documents/hf_jp-ii_spe_20010825_introd-messa.html.

115. See John Paul II, "Angelus Address, Corpus Christi, June 5, 1983," quoted in Calkins, "Our Lady's Presence in the Mass," 60.

116. Visit "The Veil Removed," produced by Brenden Stanley (Urbandale, IA: The Veil Removed, 2019), video, 7 min. https://theveilremoved.com/watch/.

117. See John 19:25.

Notes

118. René Laurentin, *Mary in Scripture, Liturgy, and the Catholic Tradition* (Paulist Press: New York/Mahwah, NJ, 2014), 94.

119. Ignatius of Loyola, "Spiritual Journal," in Simon Decloux, *Commentaries on the Letters and Spiritual Diary of St. Ignatius of Loyola* (Rome: Centrum Ignatianum Spiritualitis, 1982), 140, emphasis mine.

120. Laurentin, *Mary in Scripture, Liturgy, and the Catholic Tradition*, 94. Although Laurentin includes this insight of St. Ignatius of Loyola, later in his book he expresses his opposition to the thought of Mary's presence in the Eucharist. See p. 149.

121. Calkins, "Our Lady's Presence in the Mass," 69.

122. Brian E. Daley, *On the Dormition of Mary: Early Patristic Homilies* (Crestwood, NY: St. Vladimir's Seminary Press, 1998), 32.

123. See Laurentin, *Mary in Scripture, Liturgy, and the Catholic Tradition*, 162–67. Laurentin concludes his book on Mary with a reflection on Mary's presence in the Church.

124. See John Paul II, *Redemptoris Mater*, 24, 31.

125. Laurentin, *Mary in Scripture, Liturgy, and the Catholic Tradition*, 162. Laurentin, on the topic of Mary's presence, affirms her presence is "permanent and universal," "discreet," and an "image of Trinitarian love." See 151–59.

126. CDF, *Inter Insigniores* [On the Question of Admission of Women to the Ministerial Priesthood], October 15, 1976, 6, https://www.vatican.va/roman_curia/congregations/cfaith/documents/rc_con_cfaith_doc_19761015_inter-insigniores_en.html, emphasis mine.

Chapter 3

1. ITC, *Synodality in the Life and Mission of the Church*, 2017, 150, https://www.vatican.va/roman_curia/congregations/cfaith/cti_documents/rc_cti_20180302_sinodalita_en.html.

2. Synod of Bishops, *Vademecum for the Synod on Synodality* (Vatican City: Secretary General of the Synod of Bishops, 2021), 2.3.

3. Kevin M. Clarke, following the original Greek, translates *pondered* as *considered in her mind*. See *Divinely Given "Into Our Reality": Mary's Maternal Mediation According to Pope Benedict XVI*.

Marian Approaches to Synodality

Paper given at the Ecumenical Society of the Blessed Virgin Mary, Pittsburgh, August 13, 2008, 4. Clarke goes on to note "the word for *consider* here derives from the Greek root *dialogue*."

4. Mary's motive for questioning the angel has been compared to Zechariah's question to the angel Gabriel, "How will I know that this is so? For I am an old man, and my wife is getting on in years" (Luke 1:18). Zechariah asks this question after Gabriel reveals his wife, Elizabeth, will bear a son. Because of his doubt, Zechariah was silenced. For a brief reflection, see Andrew Swaford, "What Can We Learn from Zechariah's Doubt and Mary's Faith?" September 16, 2016, https://media.ascensionpress.com/2016/09/16/zechariahs-question-marys-faith/.

5. Cardinal Joseph Ratzinger and Hans Urs von Balthasar, *Mary: The Church at the Source* (San Francisco: Ignatius Press, 1997), 70.

6. See Luke 1:28. The NRSVCE translation of the Bible reads "favoured one," while the Douay-Rheims translation reads "full of grace."

7. Edward Sri, *Walking with Mary: A Biblical Journey from Nazareth to the Cross* (New York: Image Press, 2017), 41. See also Josh 1:9.

8. See General Secretariat of the Synod, *"Enlarge the Space of Your Tent" (Isa 54:2): Working Document for the Continental Stage* (Vatican City: October 2022), https://www.synod.va/content/dam/synod/common/phases/continental-stage/dcs/Documento-Tappa-Continentale-EN.pdf.

9. See Canadian Conference of Catholic Bishops, *Synod on Synodality: National Synthesis for Canada* (2022), https://www.cccb.ca/wp-content/uploads/2022/09/Synod-on-Synodality-EN-2022-08-31.pdf.

10. CCCB, *National Synthesis*, 1.

11. CCCB, *National Synthesis*, 3. Similarly, the final document of the Australian Conference of Bishops, *Synod of Bishops Australian Synthesis Continental Stage* (April 13, 2023), addressed the needs of indigenous people. See 57, https://s3.ap-southeast-2.amazonaws.com/acbcwebsite/Articles/Documents/ACBC/FINAL%20Australian%20Synthesis%20Report%20-%20Continental%20Stage.pdf.

12. CCCB, *National Synthesis*, 8.

13. For papal speeches during the visit to Canada, visit https://www.cccb.ca/indigenous-peoples/pope-francis-penitential-pilgrimage/speeches/.

Notes

14. CCCB, *National Synthesis*, 22.

15. USCCB, *National Synthesis of the People of God in the United States of America for the Diocesan Phase of the 2021–2023 Synod*, https://www.usccb.org/resources/US%20National%20Synthesis%202021-2023%20Synod.pdf.

16. USCCB, *National Synthesis of the People of God in the United States*, 5.

17. The *National Synthesis of the People of God in the United States* notes division regarding the celebration of the liturgy and marginalization due to "social and/or economic power, such as immigrant communities; ethnic minorities; those who are undocumented; the unborn and their mothers; people who are experiencing poverty, homelessness, or incarceration; those people who have disabilities or mental health issues; and people suffering from various addictions," 5. Other groups identified as experiencing marginalization are the LGBTQ+ community, the divorced, "or those who have remarried without a declaration of nullity, as well as those who have civilly married but who never married in the Church," 6.

18. UCCSB, *National Synthesis of the People of God in the United States*, 6.

19. See Pew Research, https://www.pewresearch.org/fact-tank/2018/10/10/7-facts-about-american-catholics/.

20. See *The Pillar*, "USCCB: Synod Process 'Not Perfect,' But Synodality Is 'Not Over,'" (September 27, 2022), https://www.pillarcatholic.com/usccb-synod-process-not-perfect-but-synodality-is-not-over/. Also, there appears to be no way of knowing whether all participants were well catechized, active in parish life, or even Catholic.

21. John of Damascus, "On the Dormition of the Holy Mother of God," in *On the Dormition of Mary: Early Patristic Homilies*, ed. Brian J. Daley (Crestwood, NY: St. Vladimir's Seminary Press, 1997), 193.

22. See Maximus the Confessor, *The Life of the Virgin*, trans. Stephen J. Shoemaker (New Haven, CT: Yale University Press, 2012), 149–51.

23. North American Synod Team, *For a Synodal Church: Communion, Participation, and Mission, North American Final Document*

for the Continental Stage of the 2021-2024 Synod (CCCB and USCCB, 2023), 23.

24. *DCS* 60.

25. *DCS* 61.

26. *North American Final Document for the Continental Stage*, 19.

27. *DCS* 64.

28. *DCS* 64, emphasis mine. Similar concerns were presented in the final document of the Australian bishops. See *Australian Synthesis Continental Stage*, 47 and 60.

29. See Susan Bigelow Reynolds, "Are We Protagonists Yet? The Place of Women in the Synodal Working Document," December 2, 2022, https://www.commonwealmagazine.org/women-church-synod-francis-catholic.

30. Sixteenth Ordinary General Assembly of the Synod of Bishops, *Instrumentum laboris*, B.2.3., June 20, 2023, https://press.vatican.va/content/salastampa/en/bollettino/pubblico/2023/06/20/230620e.html.

31. *North American Final Document for the Continental Stage*, 17. See also *Australian Synthesis Continental Stage*. After Australian participants read the *DCS*, they reported, "There was acknowledgement that more people are seeing Baptism as their common foundation for Church participation," 34.

32. *Australian Synthesis Continental Stage*, 34.

33. Susan Bigelow Reynolds, "Are We Protagonists Yet?"

34. See "Ukraine, Abortion, Racism, Women's Ordination: Highlights from *America*'s Interview with Pope Francis," November 28, 2022, *America*, https://www.americamagazine.org/faith/2022/11/28/polarization-pope-francis-america-interview-244227.

35. See John Paul II, *Mulieris Dignitatem* [Apostolic Letter on the Dignity and Vocation of Women], The Holy See, August 15, 1988, 1.

36. Apart from Church as mother, woman, and spouse, other documents, such as *Mulieris Dignitatem*, 23, 27, and 28, use Eph 5:25, referring to the Church as Bride of Christ, as another feminine model for the Church.

37. Pope Francis, "Ukraine, Abortion, Racism, Women's Ordination."

Notes

38. See John 3:29; Matt 9:15; Mark 2:19; Luke 5:34; and Rev 22:17.

39. See Eph 5:29–33. See also *CCC* 796: "The unity of Christ and the Church, head and members of one Body, also implies the distinction of the two within a personal relationship. This aspect is often expressed by the image of bridegroom and bride. The theme of Christ as Bridegroom of the Church was prepared for by the prophets and announced by John the Baptist. The Lord referred to himself as the 'bridegroom.' The Apostle speaks of the whole Church and of each of the faithful, members of his Body, as a bride 'betrothed' to Christ the Lord so as to become but one spirit with him. The Church is the spotless bride of the spotless Lamb. 'Christ loved the Church and gave himself up for her, that he might sanctify her.' He has joined her with himself in an everlasting covenant and never stops caring for her as for his own body."

40. CDF, "Letter to the Bishops of the Catholic Church on the Collaboration of Men and Women in the Church and in the World," May 31, 2004, 15, https://www.vatican.va/roman_curia/congregations/cfaith/documents/rc_con_cfaith_doc_20040731_collaboration_en.html.

41. See chapter 2.

42. See Pope Francis, "Ukraine, Abortion, Racism, Women's Ordination." Although there have been at least four Vatican commissions called to study the female diaconate in the early Church, the magisterium's teaching on the admission of women to the ministerial priesthood is found in several documents. For example, see John Paul II, *Ordinatio Sacerdotalis* [Apostolic Letter on Reserving Priestly Ordination to Men Alone], The Holy See, May 22, 1994, https://www.vatican.va/content/john-paul-ii/en/apost_letters/1994/documents/hf_jp-ii_apl_19940522_ordinatio-sacerdotalis.html. On the topic of the admission of women to the ministerial priesthood, John Paul II affirmed: "I declare that the Church has no authority whatsoever to confer *priestly ordination* on women and that this judgement is to be definitively held by all the Church's Faithful," *Ordinatio Sacerdotalis*, 4. See also CDF, *Responsum ad Propositum Dubium* [Concerning the Teaching Contained in *Ordinatio Sacerdotalis*], The Holy See, October 28, 1995, https://www.vatican.va/roman_curia/congregations/

cfaith/documents/rc_con_cfaith_doc_19951028_dubium-ordinatio-sac_en.html. In 2018, another document was issued in response to the definitive character of John Paul II's apostolic letter. See CDF, *In Response to Certain Doubts Regarding the Definitive Character of the Doctrine of* Ordinatio Sacerdotalis, The Holy See, May 29, 2018. See also Code of Canon Law, c. 1024, in *The Code of Canon Law: Latin-English Edition* (Washington, DC: Canon Law Society of America, 1983): "A baptized male alone receives sacred ordination validly."

43. See Pope Francis, "Ukraine, Abortion, Racism, Women's Ordination."

44. Pope Francis, in-flight interview, November 6, 2022, quoted in Carol Glatz, "Every Time a Woman Comes in to Do a Job in the Vatican, Things Get Better" Catholic News Service, https://www.americamagazine.org/faith/2022/11/06/pope-francis-women-rights-244098.

45. Readers' Input, *America*, December 21, 2022.

46. Readers' Input, *America*, December 21, 2022.

47. Reynolds, "Are We Protagonists Yet?"

48. Commission on Spirituality Sub-group, *Towards a Spirituality for Synodality*, 15, https://www.synod.va/en/highlights/towards-a-spirituality-for-synodality.html.

49. *IL* 20.

50. See Canon Law Society of America, *Code of Canon Law* (*Libreria Editrice Vaticana*,1989), cc. 204-231.

51. *IL* B.2.1.

52. *LG* 31 defines laity: "The term laity is here understood to mean all the faithful except those in holy orders and those in the state of religious life specially approved by the Church. These faithful are by baptism made one body with Christ and are constituted among the People of God; they are in their own way made sharers in the priestly, prophetical, and kingly functions of Christ; and they carry out for their own part the mission of the whole Christian people in the Church and in the world."

53. See "Laity, Canon Law" in *New Catholic Encyclopedia* (Gale Group, 2003).

54. See 1983 Code of Canon Law, c. 204 §1.

Notes

55. *AA* 7, emphasis mine. See also John Paul II, general audience, April 13, 1991, www.vatican.va.

56. For more on how laity are called to evangelize in the various sectors, see Josephine Lombardi, *Disciples of All Nations: A Practical Guide to the New Evangelization* (Toronto: Novalis and Twenty-Third Publications, 2014).

57. See Pope Francis, *Praedicate Evangelium*, Apostolic Constitution, March 19, 2022, Art. 14: "The officials are selected, as far as possible, from various regions of the world, so that the Curia may reflect the universal character of the Church. They are taken from among clerics, members of Institutes of Consecrated Life and Societies of Apostolic Life and the laity, who are distinguished for their experience, proven expertise attested by appropriate academic degrees, virtue and prudence. They should be chosen by objective and transparent criteria, and should have a suitable number of years of pastoral experience." https://www.vatican.va/content/francesco/en/apost_constitutions/documents/20220319-costituzione-ap-praedicate-evangelium.html.

58. John Paul II, post-synodal apostolic exhortation *Christifidelis Laici* [On the Vocation and Mission of the Lay Faithful in the Church and in the World], 1988, 59, https://www.vatican.va/content/john-paul-ii/en/apost_exhortations/documents/hf_jp-ii_exh_30121988_christifideles-laici.html.

59. Pope Francis, *Querida Amazonia* [post-synodal apostolic exhortation on the Amazon] (2020), 99.

60. See Congregation for the Clergy, Pontifical Council for the Laity, Congregation for the Doctrine of the Faith, Congregation for Divine Worship and the Discipline of the Sacraments, Congregation for Bishops, Congregation for the Evangelization of Peoples, Congregation for the Institution of Consecrated Life and Societies of Apostolic Life, Pontifical Council for the Interpretation of Legislative Texts, *Instruction On Certain Questions Regarding the Collaboration of the Non-Ordained Faithful in the Sacred Ministry of Priest*, Liberia Editrice Vaticana, 1997, https://www.vatican.va/roman_curia/congregations/cclergy/documents/rc_con_interdic_doc_15081997_en.html.

61. See *Instruction on Certain Questions Regarding Collaboration*, 1. The document explains the uniqueness of the ministerial

priesthood: "To base the foundations of the ordained ministry on Apostolic Succession, because this ministry continues the mission received by the Apostles from Christ, is an essential point of Catholic ecclesiological doctrine."

62. CCCB, *Program for Priestly Formation*, 2022, 63; cf. *LG* 10.

63. C. 861, §1: "The ordinary minister of baptism is a bishop, a presbyter, or a deacon, without prejudice to the prescript of can. 530, n. 1." §2: "When an ordinary minister is absent or impeded, a catechist or another person designated for this function by the local ordinary, or in a case of necessity any person with the right intention, confers baptism licitly. Pastors of souls, especially the pastor of a parish, are to be concerned that the Christian faithful are taught the correct way to baptize."

64. See *Instruction on Certain Questions Regarding Collaboration*. Although the respective Vatican offices underscored the need for lay assistance, they caution against confusion regarding the rights, roles, and obligations of the lay faithful: "Since these tasks are most closely linked to the duties of pastors (which office requires reception of the sacrament of Orders), it is necessary that all who are in any way involved in this collaboration, exercise particular care to safeguard the nature and mission of sacred ministry and the vocation and secular character of the lay faithful. It must be remembered that "collaboration with" does not, in fact, mean "substitution for" (Introduction).

65. See c. 766: Laypersons can be permitted to preach in a church or oratory, if necessity requires it in certain circumstances or it seems advantageous in particular cases, according to the prescripts of the conference of bishops and without prejudice to c. 767, §1. Among the forms of preaching, the homily, which is part of the liturgy itself and is reserved to a priest or deacon, is preeminent; in the homily the mysteries of faith and the norms of Christian life are to be explained from the sacred text during the liturgical year.

66. C. 767.

67. USCCB, *Decree of Promulgation* (Instruction on Lay Preaching: Complementary Norms), 2001, https://www.usccb.org/beliefs-and-teachings/what-we-believe/canon-law/complementary-norms/canon-766-lay-preaching. See also Patricia A. Parachini, *Lay Preaching: State of the Question* (Collegeville, MN: Liturgical Press, 1999). See also Lombardi, *Disciples of All Nations*, 70–77. See also CCCB, *Complementary*

Notes

Norms to the 1983 Code of Canon Law, Ottawa, 1996, https://www.cccb.ca/letter/complementary-norms-to-the-1983-code-of-canon-law/.

68. See the research of Sr. Mary Catherine Hilkert, OP, "Who Is Called to Preach the Gospel?" https://domlife.org/wp-content/uploads/2014/12/hilkert_anointedmission_en.pdf.

69. Maximus the Confessor, *Life of the Virgin*, 124.

70. 1 Cor 12:7, 8, 10.

71. This comes from *apostolos*, meaning one sent with a message. Mary Magdalene was sent to give the message of the resurrection to the apostles.

72. See Mark 16:9–11; Luke 24:1–12; John 20:1–18.

73. Pope Francis, Easter Monday Address, April 10, 2023, Catholic News Service.

74. See Roch A. Kereszty, *Jesus Christ: Fundamentals of Christology* (New York: Alba House, 2002), 46.

75. See Carolyn Pirtle, "Celebrating Mary Magdalene, Apostle to the Apostles," July 22, 2020, https://mcgrathblog.nd.edu/celebrating-mary-magdalene-apostle-to-the-apostles.

76. See Walburga Storch, ed. *Prayers of Hildegard of Bingen*, trans. Sharon Therese Nemeth (Cincinnati: St. Anthony Messenger Press, 1989), 2.

77. See Pope Paul VI, "Catherine of Siena: The Gift of Wisdom," in *The Pope Speaks* (New York: Meredith Press, 1970), 196–202.

78. Josephine Lombardi, workshop on lay preaching, June of 2020, as part of the St. Augustine's Seminary conference on preaching. The workshop is available on the video page of www.josephinelombardi.com.

79. Pope Francis, *Querida Amazonia*, 100. Pope Francis writes, "This summons us to broaden our vision, lest we restrict our understanding of the Church to her functional structures. Such a reductionism would lead us to believe that women would be granted a greater status and participation in the Church only if they were admitted to Holy Orders. But that approach would in fact narrow our vision; it would lead us to clericalize women, diminish the great value of what they have already accomplished, and subtly make their indispensable contribution less effective."

80. For more on the rights and obligations of the lay faithful, see Part 1 of Book 2 of the *New Code of Canon Law*.

81. See *DCS* 5.

82. See https://www.youtube.com/watch?v=k5oPj2UCF6U, a video including the commentary of fourteen women on women and the synodal process.

83. *AA* 1. Nine of sixteen documents of the Second Vatican Council (1962–1965) affirm the role and contribution of the laity to the mission of the Church, to evangelize and catechize future generations of Catholics and potential converts. See Second Vatican Council, Dogmatic Constitution on the Nature of the Church, 33 and following; *AAS* 57 (1965), 39 and following; see also Constitution on the Liturgy, 26–40; *AAS* 56 (1964), 107–11; see also Decree on Instruments of Social Communication: *AAS* 56 (1964), 145–58; Decree on Ecumenism: *AAS* 57 (1965), 90–107; Decree on Pastoral Duties of Bishops, 16–18; Declaration on Christian Education, 3, 5, and 7; Decree on Missionary Activity of Church, 15, 21, and 41; Decree on Priestly Life and Ministry, 9.

84. Pope John Paul II maintained and confirmed the magisterium's commitment to lay formation in his postsynodal apostolic exhortation, *Christifideles Laici*, On the Vocation and Mission of the Lay Faithful in the Church and the World (1988). See 1.

85. Center for Applied Research in the Apostolate, *Lay Ecclesial Ministers in the United States*, February 2015, https://cara.georgetown.edu/cara-research-archives.

86. See Gudran Sailer, "10 Years of Pope Francis: Significantly More Women Working at the Vatican," March 8, 2023, Vatican News, https://www.vaticannews.va/en/pope/news/2023-03/pope-francis-10-years-women-vatican.html.

87. 1983 *CIC* 246 § 3 Encourages devotion to Mary in seminary life: "Devotion to the Blessed Virgin Mary, including the rosary, mental prayer and other devotional exercises are to be fostered so that the students acquire a spirit of prayer and gain strength in their vocation."

88. Pope John Paul II, *MD* 31, emphasis mine. By emphasizing "all the manifestations of the feminine genius," this could be used to affirm the diversity of women, their unique personalities and use of gifts.

Notes

89. See Pope John Paul II, "Final Message to Participants of Lourdes Pilgrimage," August 15, 2004. See also Melissa Maleski, *The Supreme Vocation of Women According to John Paul II* (Bedford, NH: Sophia Institute Press, 2020).

90. Pope Francis, Address to Permanent Deacons, June 19, 2021.

91. Pope Francis, general audience, April 15, 2015. He made a similar point in his interview with America Media, dated November 22, 2022.

92. See Lisa Cotter, *Reveal the Gift: Living the Feminine Genius* (West Chester, PA: Ascension Press, 2022). Cotter explains that the expression "feminine genius" refers to receptivity, maternity, sensitivity, and generosity.

93. Pope Francis, interview, *America*, November 28, 2022.

94. Leonardo Boff, *The Maternal Face of God* (London: Collins Religious Publications, 1989), 11.

95. Kevin M. Clarke, "Divinely Given 'Into Our Reality': Mary's Maternal Mediation according to Pope Benedict XVI," Ecumenical Society of the Blessed Virgin Mary, Pittsburgh, August 13, 2008, 10, https://www.academia.edu/12334203/_Divinely_Given_Into_Our_Reality_Mary_s_Maternal_Mediation_according_to_Pope_Benedict_XVI_Ecumenical_Society_of_the_Blessed_Virgin_Mary_Pittsburgh_Aug_13_2008.

96. See Salvatore Cernuzio, "Vatican Produces Liturgical Rite for Institution of Catechists," *Vatican News*, December 13, 2021, https://www.vaticannews.va/en/vatican-city/news/2021-12/vatican-produces-liturgical-rite-for-institution-of-catechists.html.

97. Cernuzio, "Vatican Produces Liturgical Rite for Institution of Catechists." See also Pope Francis, *Antiquum Ministerium* [Instituting the Ministry of the Catechist], May 10, 2021, https://www.vatican.va/content/francesco/en/motu_proprio/documents/papa-francesco-motu-proprio-20210510_antiquum-ministerium.html.

98. Congregation for Divine Worship and the Discipline of the Sacraments, "Letter to the Presidents of the Episcopal Conferences on the Rite of Institution of Catechists," December 3, 2021, n. 4, https://www.vatican.va/roman_curia/congregations/ccdds/documents/rc

_con_ccdds_doc_20211203_lettera-rito-istituzione-catechisti_en.html.

99. N. 10 includes an additional exercise: "The Bishop delegates "truly worthy and suitably prepared" Catechists to celebrate the Minor Exorcisms." For more on an explanation of major and minor exorcisms see https://www.usccb.org/prayer-and-worship/sacraments-and-sacramentals/sacramentals-blessings/exorcism.

100. Courtney Mares, "Pope Francis Confers Lay Ministries upon Ten People in St. Peter's Basilica," Catholic News Agency, January 22, 2023, https://www.catholicnewsagency.com/news/253425/pope-francis-confers-lay-ministries-upon-ten-people-in-st-peter-s-basilica.

101. See Pope Paul VI, *Motu Proprio, Ministeria Quaedam*, 1972.

102. See Maximus the Confessor, *Life of the Virgin*. Translator and commentator Stephen J. Shoemaker notes the presence of other accounts of the life of Mary, including a text by John Geometres, a Byzantine monk and poet.

103. See Ally Kateusz, *Mary and Early Christian Women: Hidden Leadership* (Cham, Switzerland: Palgrave/Macmillan, 2019).

104. *DCS* 60.

105. See *LG* 19, 20, and ITC, "Catholic Teaching on Apostolic Succession," 1973, 3, https://www.vatican.va/roman_curia/congregations/cfaith/cti_documents/rc_cti_1973_successione-apostolica_en.html.

106. Pope Paul VI, *Marialus Cultus* [For the Right Ordering and Development of Devotion to the Blessed Virgin Mary], The Holy See, February 2, 1974, 18, https://www.vatican.va/content/paul-vi/en/apost_exhortations/documents/hf_p-vi_exh_19740202_marialis-cultus.html.

107. Maximus the Confessor, *Life of the Virgin*, 102. Compare Matt 27:55, emphasis mine.

108. See Pope Benedict XVI, apostolic letter *Motu Proprio, Omnium in Mentem*, On Several Amendments to the Code of Canon Law, October 26, 2009. Canon 1008 no longer includes all degrees of Holy Orders as acting *in persona Christi*. Paragraph 3 of Canon 1009 was added to read: "Those who are constituted in the order of the epis-

Notes

copate or the presbyterate receive the mission and capacity to act in the person of Christ the Head, whereas deacons are empowered to serve the People of God in the ministries of the liturgy, the word and charity." The earlier version did not contain the third paragraph distinguishing between deacon, priest, and bishop. See also *CCC* 1548.

109. See von Thomas Schüller, 'In Persona Mariae,' *Herder Communications* 5 (2020): 41–43. Schüller proposes women, acting *in persona Mariae*, bring Mary's tenderness to ministry.

110. For more, see Cardinal Joseph Ratzinger, *Daughter Zion: Meditations on the Church's Marian Belief* (San Francisco: Ignatius Press, 1983). According to Ratzinger, Mary as Daughter Zion represents God's intimacy with Israel, calling her to be pure, faithful, and fruitful. Here fruitfulness is not limited to procreation. See also *RM* 3.

111. The ministry of early female deacons, women who ministered to women in the early Church is well documented. In the early Church, among other activities, women prepared other women for baptism and ministered to sick and dying women. For obvious reasons, men could not anoint the bodies of women, preparing them for baptism. Rom 16:1 refers to Phoebe, a deacon. See ITC, *From the Diakonia of Christ to the Diakonia of the Apostles*, 2002. In May 2016, the UISG-USG asked Pope Francis to call a commission to study the permanent diaconate that existed in the early Church. The pope agreed but declared that the research of this commission was inconclusive. During his final address at the conclusion of the Special Synod of Bishops of the Pan-Amazon Region, Pope Francis indicated he was open to reconvening a new commission. On April 8, 2020, Pope Francis announced the names of the members of the new commission, the research of which has yet to be shared. See https://www.vaticannews.va/en/pope/news/2020-04/pope-commission-women-deacons.html.

112. See CDF, *Inter Insigniores* [On the Question of Admission of Women to the Ministerial Priesthood], The Holy See, October 15, 1976, 5, https://www.vatican.va/roman_curia/congregations/cfaith/documents/rc_con_cfaith_doc_19761015_inter-insigniores_en.html. See also John Paul II, *Ordinatio Sacerdotialis*, May 22, 1994, The Holy

Marian Approaches to Synodality

See, 2, https://www.vatican.va/content/john-paul-ii/en/apost_letters/1994/documents/hf_jp-ii_apl_19940522_ordinatio-sacerdotalis.html.

113. The NRSV includes the variant "of the women" in a footnote on the psalm.

114. Letter to the Presidents of the Episcopal Conferences on the Rite of Institution of Catechists, n. 13.

115. See *CCC* 1537. In past decades, some women have become consecrated virgins. For more, see Catholic News Agency, "The Little-Known Vocation of Consecrated Virginity," November 10, 2017, https://www.catholicnewsagency.com/news/37170/the-little-known-vocation-of-consecrated-virginity.

116. See Lynn H. Cohick and Amy Brown Hughes, *Christian Women in the Patristic World: Their Influence, Authority, and Legacy in the Second through Fifth Centuries* (Grand Rapids, MI: Baker Academic, 2017), 67–69.

117. See Richard Gaillardetz, "Ecclesiological Foundations of Ministry in an Ordered Communion," in *Ordering the Baptismal Priesthood*, ed. Susan K. Wood (Minnesota: Liturgical Press, 2003), 46. Here Gaillardetz refers to the research of Marcel Metzger on the *Apostolic Constitutions*. See Marcel Metzger, "Ministères, ordinations, clergé et people dans les 'Constitutions Apostoliques," in *Ordination et Ministères* (Rome: Edizioni Liturgiche, 1995), 209.

118. I designed a model for lay preaching. A video with the breakdown can be found on the video page of my website, www.josephinelombardi.com.

119. Pastoral Commission of the Sacred Congregation for the Evangelization of Peoples, "The Role of Women in Evangelization," 1976, in *Vatican Council II: More Post Conciliar Documents* (Northport, NY: Costello, 1982), 318–30.

120. "Role of Women in Evangelization," 319. Cf. *AG* 35a.

121. "Role of Women in Evangelization," 320.

122. "Role of Women in Evangelization," 320.

123. See William Weber, "Saint Paul and Apostolic Succession," *The Monist* 10, no. 4 (1900): 516. Although Weber distinguishes between the mission of "the Twelve" and the mission of St. Paul and "many more apostles," Acts 13:3 acknowledges St. Paul receiving the laying on of hands and Acts 19:1–6, 1 Tim 4:14, and 2 Tim 1:6 doc-

Notes

ument St. Paul laying hands on others, including Timothy. See also *CCC* 1590.

124. "Role of Women in Evangelization," 321.

125. "Role of Women in Evangelization," 326. Cf. *AG* 40.

126. "Role of Women in Evangelization," 325. The document authors include a footnote explaining *diakonia* as a service, "not the same as the order of the diaconate."

127. For more on the first and new evangelization, see Lombardi, *Disciples of All Nations*.

128. See Gaillardetz, "Ecclesiological Foundations of Ministry," 36.

129. Christian women from other ecclesial communities have made great progress in this area. Examples include Joyce Meyer, Beth Moore, Lisa Bevere, and Christine Caine, to name a few.

130. There is an apostolate of "Spiritual Motherhood of Priests" that was founded in Ottawa, Canada. The inspiration for the apostolate is found on the "About Us" page of the apostolate's website. On December 8, 2007, the Solemnity of the Immaculate Conception, a document from the Congregation for the Clergy was sent to all the bishops of the world. It was titled "Eucharistic Adoration for the Sanctification of Priests and Spiritual Maternity." In essence, the letter requested that women spiritually adopt priests and embrace Eucharistic adoration, in a spirit of genuine reparation and purification, for the sanctification of priests. In an answer to this call, our apostolate of "Spiritual Motherhood of Priests" was conceived. Visit https://spiritualmotherhoodofpriests.ca/about-us/.

131. See "What is Magnificat?" https://magnificat-ministry.net/home/what-is-magnificat/. Magnificat, A Ministry to Catholic Women is a private association of the Christian faithful under the jurisdiction of the local ordinary (c. 305.2). Its purpose is to help Catholic women to open more and more to the Holy Spirit through a deeper commitment of their lives to Jesus as Lord and to impart the Holy Spirit to one another by their love, service, and sharing the good news of salvation. It thus provides opportunities that will foster a desire to grow in holiness.

132. See https://dynamicwomenfaith.com/mission/.

133. See https://www.wowblessingstoronto.com.

Marian Approaches to Synodality

134. For many years, I served as a Project Rachel counselor in the Diocese of Hamilton, Canada. Project Rachel is a ministry for women who need post-abortion counseling. These women appreciate going to other women for pastoral care. Rachel's Vineyard is a similar ministry.

135. After the premiere of my film, *The First Lady and Her Successors*, a priest wrote to me saying, "It never occurred to me that women can relate to Mary."

136. The *Document for the Continental Stage* includes this statement by a participant in the synodal consultations: "I distrust the Synod. I think it has been called to bring about further change to Christ's teachings and wound his Church further" (individual submission from the United Kingdom).

137. See Christopher White, "Pope Francis Using Synods to Build Consensus in Church, Participant Says," October 3, 2019, Crux, https://cruxnow.com/vatican/2019/10/pope-francis-using-synods-to-build-consensus-in-church-participant-says.

138. See International Marian Association, *The Role of Mary in Redemption: A Document of the Theological Commission of the International Marian Association*, 2017. The document concludes with this request: "Therefore, we, as members of the Theological Commission of the International Marian Association, and in full obedience and fidelity to our Holy Father, Pope Francis, humbly request that during this 2017 Fatima centenary, and in continuity with the papal precedents of Pope Pius XI and Pope St. John Paul II, Pope Francis would kindly grant public recognition and honor to the role of the Blessed Virgin Mary for her unique human cooperation with the one divine Redeemer in the work of Redemption as **"Co-redemptrix with Jesus the Redeemer."** We believe that a public acknowledgement of Mary's true and continuous role with Jesus in the saving work of Redemption would justly celebrate the role of humanity in God's saving plan and lead to the release of historic graces through an even more powerful exercise of Our Lady's maternal roles of intercession for the Church and for all humanity today." https://internationalmarian.com/sites/marian/files/uploads/documents/the_role_of_mary_in_redemption_1.pdf.

139. Boff, *The Maternal Face of God*, 5.

Notes

Chapter 4

1. Stephen Covey, *The 7 Habits of Highly Effective People* (New York: Simon & Schuster, 1989).

2. Pope Benedict XVI, homily, The Holy See, September 11, 2006, https://www.vatican.va/content/benedict-xvi/en/homilies/2006/documents/hf_ben-xvi_hom_20060911_shrine-altotting.html.

3. Kevin M. Clarke, "Divinely Given 'Into Our Reality': Mary's Maternal Mediation according to Pope Benedict XVI," Ecumenical Society of the Blessed Virgin Mary, Pittsburgh, Aug. 13, 2008, 6, https://www.academia.edu/12334203/_Divinely_Given_Into_Our_Reality_Mary_s_Maternal_Mediation_according_to_Pope_Benedict_XVI_Ecumenical_Society_of_the_Blessed_Virgin_Mary_Pittsburgh_Aug_13_2008.

4. See Charles Journet, "The Trial of Separation," in *The Mary Book* (London: Sheed & Ward, 1950), 123.

5. Sofia Cavalletti, *Ebraismo e Spiritualità Cristiana* (Rome: Editrice Studium, 1966), 50.

6. Adrienne von Speyr, *Handmaid of the Lord* (San Francisco: Ignatius Press, 1985), 104.

7. The USCCB Synthesis reports only 700,000 participants responded to the consultation, about 10 percent of Catholics. Pew Research indicates there are roughly fifty-one million Catholics in the United States of America. See https://www.pewresearch.org/fact-tank/2018/10/10/7-facts-about-american-catholics/.

8. *DCS* 5, https://www.synod.va/content/dam/synod/common/phases/continental-stage/dcs/Documento-Tappa-Continentale-EN.pdf.

9. *DCS* 36. These same issues resurfaced in the *North American Final Document for the Continental Stage of the 2021–2024 Synod*, April 12, 2023, 26, https://www.usccb.org/resources/North%20American%20Final%20Document%20-%20English.pdf. See also Australian Catholic Bishops' Conference, *Synod of Bishops Australian Synthesis Continental Stage*, April 13, 2023, 44, www.catholic.org.au/synodalchurch.

10. Josephine Lombardi, "Mercy and Beyond: Pope Francis' Marian Program of Life," 5. Quote from Bull of Indiction *Misericordiae Vultus*, 2. Quote from *EG* 112.

Marian Approaches to Synodality

11. USCCB, *National Synthesis of the People of God in the United States of America for the Diocesan Phase of the 2021–2023 Synod*, 7, https://www.usccb.org/resources/US%20National%20Synthesis%202021-2023%20Synod.pdf.

12. USCCB, *National Synthesis*, 7.

13. See the Synodal Path of the German Bishops, Documents, https://www.synodalerweg.de/english/documents. To date, there have been four forums: 1. Power and Separation of Powers in the Church—Joint Participation and Involvement in the Mission; 2. Priestly Existence Today; 3. Women in Ministries and Offices in the Church; 4. Life in Succeeding Relationships—Living Love in Sexuality and Partnership.

14. Statement of the Holy See on German "Synodal Way." Catholic News Agency, working translation into English, July 22, 2022. For original in Italian see https://press.vatican.va/content/salastampa/it/bollettino/pubblico/2022/07/21/0550/01133.html#de.

15. See https://www.vaticannews.va/en/vatican-city/news/2022-07/holy-see-germany-church-synodal-path-convergence-universal-churc.html.

16. Austin Ivereigh, "I Helped Write the First Global Synod Document. Here's What We Heard from Catholics around the World," *America*, October 27, 2022, https://www.americamagazine.org/faith/2022/10/27/frascati-document-synod-synodality-244031.

17. Ivereigh, "I Helped Write the First Global Synod Document."

18. Claire Giangravé, "Meet Sr. Nathalie Becquart, the Woman Who Is Helping Reshape the Catholic Church," *Global Sisters Report* (December 9, 2021), https://www.globalsistersreport.org/news/news/news/meet-sr-nathalie-becquart-woman-who-helping-reshape-catholic-church.

19. See Federation of Asian Bishops' Conference, *Final Document of the Asian Continental Assembly on Synodality*, March 16, 2023, 64–66, 95–97, https://fabc.org/wp-content/uploads/2023/03/ACAS-Final-Document-16-Mar-2023.pdf.

20. Susan Bigelow Reynolds, "Are We Protagonists Yet? The Place of Women in the Synodal Working Document," December 2,

Notes

2022, https://www.commonwealmagazine.org/women-church-synod-francis-catholic.

21. *UISG-USG Contribution to the Synod on Synodality III*, 2, https://www.usgroma.org/l/sinodality-gods-dream/.

22. See Jose Kavi, "Religious Leaders, Women in India Struggle with Clergy Abuse of Nuns," *Global Sisters Report,* June 24, 2016, https://www.globalsistersreport.org/news/equality/religious-leaders-women-india-struggle-clergy-abuse-nuns-40571.

23. See Carol Glatz, "Every Time a Woman Comes in to Do a Job in the Vatican, Things Get Better," Catholic News Service, November 11, 2006, https://www.americamagazine.org/faith/2022/11/06/pope-francis-women-rights-244098.

24. Ivereigh, "I Helped Write the First Global Synod Document."

25. See CCCB, *National Synthesis,* 39, and CCCB and USCCB, *North American Final Document,* 10.

26. See Josephine Lombardi, "Discerning a Priestly Vocation: Toward a Program of Integral Human Formation," in *Vocations and Prayer: The Catholic Magazine on Vocation Ministry* 28, no. 115 (July–September 2019): 3, 7–10. Permission granted to reproduce content from the article. This article inspired me to create a new program. The content of this article has evolved into a human formation educational program for the propaedeutic year of priestly formation. A companion program created for the laity, The Experts in Humanity Project,™ can be found on my website, www.josephinelombardi.com.

27. See the research of Bessel van der Kolk, *The Body Keeps the Score* (New York: Penguin Books, 2014).

28. For more on how to include women as Marian successors in seminary formation, see Josephine Lombardi, "*In Persona Mariae*: Another Mary for Another Christ in Seminary Formation" in *For the Love of the Church,* ed. Peter Lovrick (Toronto: Novalis, 2022), 315–41. See also Simon Mary of the Cross, MCarm, "Seminary Life and Formation under Mary's Mantle: An Exploration of Mary's Mission and Presence in Initial Priestly Formation." Thesis completed in partial fulfillment of the requirements for the degree Licentiate of Sacred Theology, University of Dayton, 2019.

29. The CCCB and the USCCB have prepared national-level *Rationes* for their respective nations.

30. See Australian Conference of Bishops, *Synod of Bishops Australian Synthesis Continental Stage*, April 13, 2023, 66, https://mediablog.catholic.org.au/australian-synthesis-for-global-synod-of-bishops-published/.

31. Raju Hasmukh, "Abuse Expert: Women Must Be Included in Formation of Priests," *Gaudium Press* English Edition, November 6, 2022, https://www.gaudiumpress.ca/abuse-expert-women-must-be-included-in-formation-of-priests/.

32. Hasmukh, "Abuse Expert."

33. For more on factors that influence human behavior, see Josephine Lombardi, *Experts in Humanity: A Journey of Self-Discovery and Healing* (Toronto: Novalis, 2016). In 2017 *Experts in Humanity* was awarded first place in the category of Family Life by the Catholic Press Association of the United States and Canada.

34. See Alice Miller, *The Body Never Lies* (New York: W. W. Norton, 2004), 6, 89, 92, 146, 175, 200–06. On page 6 she writes, "looks expressing disapproval and rejection that is directed at the infant can contribute to the development of severe disturbances."

35. Miller, *The Body Never Lies*, 259.

36. See Miller, *The Body Never Lies*, 89, 92.

37. See Pope Emeritus Benedict XVI, "The Church and the Scandal of Sexual Abuse," Catholic News Agency, April 10, 2019, https://www.catholicnewsagency.com/news/41013/full-text-of-benedict-xvi-essay-the-church-and-the-scandal-of-sexual-abuse.

38. See, for example, Pope Francis, Video Message of the Holy Father Francis for the Meeting Our Common Mission of Safeguarding God's Children, September 19–22, 2021, https://www.vatican.va/content/francesco/en/messages/pont-messages/2021/documents/20210918-videomessaggio-incontro-tutela-minori.html. Pope Francis said, "Rather, only by facing the truth of these evil practices and of humbly seeking pardon from victims and survivors will the Church find its way to a place where it can be relied upon once again as a place of welcome and safety for those in need. Our expressions of sorrow must be converted into concrete pathways of reform to both prevent

further abuse and to give confidence to others that our efforts will bring about real and reliable change."

40. Fr. Hans Zollner, SJ, resigned from the Pontifical Commission for the Protection of Minors on March 29, 2023. He cited concerns regarding "structural and practical issues" with the commission. See Hans Zollner, SJ, March 29, 2023. "Statement by Father Hans Zollner SJ," tweet, https://twitter.com/hans_zollner/status/1641080355405942784. Similarly, Baroness Hollins, an expert in child psychiatry and psychotherapy, and one of the first members to be appointed to the Pontifical Commission for the Protection of Minors, worked alongside victims of abuse, advising the Church on how to manage these issues. See Christopher Lamb, "Baroness Hollins Challenges Effectiveness of Vatican Child Protection Body," *The Tablet*, December 13, 2022. The recent reform has placed the Pontifical Commission for the Protection of Minors under the Dicastery for the Doctrine of the Faith. See Pope Francis, Apostolic Constitution, *Praedicate Evangelium* [On the Roman Curia and its Service to the Church in the World], The Holy See, March 19, 2022, https://www.vatican.va/content/francesco/en/apost_constitutions/documents/20220319-costituzione-ap-praedicate-evangelium.html. Main Vatican departments are now known as dicasteries.

41. Miller, *The Body Never Lies*, 201.

42. Miller, *The Body Never Lies*, 7.

43. In 1997, the USCCB prepared a document for parents of same-sex attracted youth, "Always Our Children." In 2006, the bishops updated their approach with a new document with guidelines for pastoral care: Ministry to Persons with a Homosexual Inclination: Guidelines for Pastoral Care. Visit https://www.usccb.org/resources/always-our-children.

44. Pope Francis addresses this issue in *Amoris Laetitia*, 243: "It is important that the divorced who have entered a new union should be made to feel part of the Church. They are not excommunicated.

And they should not be treated as such, since they remain part of the ecclesial community."

45. The Archdiocese of Toronto offers a ministry to widowed, separated, and divorced individuals, "New Beginnings." Similarly, the Diocese of Hamilton, also in Canada, offers a Levels Program for the same demographic. For adult children of divorce, the ministry "Life-Giving Wounds" has proven to be very helpful. Visit https://www.lifegivingwounds.org.

46. See Lombardi, *Experts in Humanity*, 66.

47. See Lombardi, *Experts in Humanity*, for more detail, including research on these issues.

48. For example, The Experts in Humanity Project™ that I created offers formation for seminarians and the laity. See www.josephinelombardi.com for details. See also Marysia Weber, *The Art of Accompaniment: Practical Steps for the Seminary Formator* (St. Louis: En Route, 2018).

49. See *EG* 169.

50. See Colleen Campbell and Thomas Carani, *The Art of Accompaniment: Theological, Spiritual, and Practical Elements of Building a More Relational Church* (Washington: Catholic Apostolate Center, 2019).

51. For more on fatherhood, see Josephine Lombardi, *On Earth as It Is in Heaven: Jubilee Edition* (Toronto: Novalis, 2023).

52. Listen to podcast found at https://www.npr.org/2020/08/14/902522133/sister-helen-prejean-on-witnessing-executions-i-couldn-t-let-them-die-alone.

53. See https://sistersoflife.org/who-we-are/who-we-are/.

54. Canada's euthanasia laws are some of the most extreme in the world.

55. Pope John Paul II, excerpt from Prayer for the Marian Year 1987–88.

Chapter 5

1. *DCS* 88.
2. The New Jerusalem Bible (New York: Doubleday, 1989).

Notes

3. Holy Bible Douay-Rheims Version (Charlotte, NC: Saint Benedict Press, 1899).

4. Migrants and Refugees Section of the Dicastery for Promoting Integral Human Development, *Doing Theology from the Existential Peripheries*, The Holy See, https://migrants-refugees.va/theology-from-the-peripheries/.

5. *Doing Theology*.

6. On November 10, 2022, the University of St. Michael's College in Toronto, Canada, hosted the Synod Panel on Listening to People on the Peripheries Conference, with a presentation of the project, including members of the project team who shared their experiences. Fr. Stan Chu Ilo, in his remarks, commented that the synod was extended due to the report submitted by his team.

7. North American Synod Team, *North American Final Document for the Continental Stage of the 2021–2024 Synod*, April 12, 2023, 22, https://www.usccb.org/resources/North%20American%20Final%20Document%20-%20English.pdf. Similarly, the final document of the Australian Bishops includes commentary on the need to reach out to those in the peripheries. See Australian Conference of Bishops, *Synod of Bishops Australian Synthesis Continental Stage* (April 13, 2023), 44, https://s3.ap-southeast-2.amazonaws.com/acbcwebsite/Articles/Documents/ACBC/FINAL%20Australian%20Synthesis%20Report%20-%20Continental%20Stage.pdf.

8. See Pope Francis, *Veritatis Gaudium* [On Ecclesiastical Universities and Faculties], The Holy See, December 27, 2017, 6, https://www.vatican.va/content/francesco/en/apost_constitutions/documents/papa-francesco_costituzione-ap_20171208_veritatis-gaudium.html.

9. I interviewed Dr. Matthia Langone for my film, *The First Lady and Her Successors*. Dr. Langone provided commentary for the mystery of the Visitation. Her icon, *The Recognition*, depicts the encounter between Mary and Elizabeth. To view the film and Dr. Langone's commentary, visit www.josephinelombardi.com.

10. Ministries that offer support to those experiencing homelessness, like the De Mazenod Door Outreach, in Hamilton, Ontario, Canada, provide respite and relief to those in need of comfort and resources. Visit http://demazenod-door.ca.

Marian Approaches to Synodality

11. Fr. Stan Chu Ilo, project member, during the conference Doing Theology from the Peripheries, held at the University of St. Michael's College in Toronto, Canada, on November 10, 2022.

12. See Hamilton Health Sciences, "The Other Side of Covid-19: Mental Health Challenges Prevalent in Youth," March 15, 2021, https://www.hamiltonhealthsciences.ca/share/youth-mental-health-during-covid-19/.

13. Hamilton Health Sciences, "The Other Side of Covid-19."

14. Fr. Stan Chu Ilo, Doing Theology from the Peripheries.

15. Dietrich Bonhoeffer, *Meditations on the Cross*, trans. Douglas W. Scott (Westminster John Knox Press: Louisville, Kentucky, 1996), 27.

16. Bonhoeffer, *Meditations on the Cross*, 7.

17. Commission on Spirituality Sub-group, *Towards a Spirituality for Synodality*, 51, https://www.synod.va/en/highlights/towards-a-spirituality-for-synodality.html.

18. Pope Benedict XVI, *Deus Caritas Est*, The Holy See, December 25, 2005, 42, https://www.vatican.va/content/benedict-xvi/en/encyclicals/documents/hf_ben-xvi_enc_20051225_deus-caritas-est.html.

19. See Martin Luther King Jr., "I've Been to the Mountaintop," April 3, 1968, https://www.google.com/search?client=safari&rls=en&q=ive+been+to+the+mountaintop&ie=UTF-8&oe=UTF-8.

20. See Pope John Paul II, encyclical letter *Redemptoris Mater*, The Holy See, March 25, 1987, 18.

21. The Greek word for "sword" here is *rhomphaia*, meaning a large double-edged sword.

22. Maximus the Confessor, *The Life of the Virgin*, trans. Stephen J. Shoemaker (New Haven, CT: Yale University Press, 2012), 30.

23. See chapter 2.

24. John Paul II, *Salvifici Doloris* [Apostolic Letter on the Christian Meaning of Human Suffering], The Holy See, February 11, 1984, 30, https://www.vatican.va/content/john-paul-ii/en/apost_letters/1984/documents/hf_jp-ii_apl_11021984_salvifici-doloris.html.

25. Pope Benedict XVI, general audience, "Connection between the Blessed Virgin Mary and the Priesthood," August 12, 2009, https://www.vatican.va/content/benedict-xvi/en/audiences/2009/documents/hf_ben-xvi_aud_20090812.html.

Notes

26. Benedict XVI, "Connection between the Blessed Virgin Mary and the Priesthood."

27. Benedict XVI, homily, Solemnity of the Mother of God, January 1, 2007.

Chapter 6

1. See ITC, *From the Diakonia of Christ to the Diakonia of the Apostles*, The Holy See, 2002, 3.

2. Preparatory Document, *For a Synodal Church: Communion, Participation, and Mission*, September 7, 2021, 32, https://www.synod.va/en/news/the-preparatory-document.html, citing Pope Francis, Address at the Opening of the Synod of Bishops of Young People, October 3, 2018.

3. Jos Moons, "A Comprehensive Introduction to Synodality: Reconfiguring Ecclesiology and Ecclesial Practice," *Annals of Theology* 69, no. 2 (2022): 90.

4. Moons, "A Comprehensive Introduction to Synodality," 90.

5. John Paul II referred to Mary as the "Star of the New Evangelization" in the apostolic exhortation *Ecclesia in America*, The Holy See, January 22, 1999, 11, https://www.vatican.va/content/john-paul-ii/en/apost_exhortations/documents/hf_jp-ii_exh_22011999_ecclesia-in-america.html.

6. There are four Marian dogmas: Mary, Ever Virgin; Mary, Mother of God; the Immaculate Conception; and the Assumption.

7. Apart from this inquiry, in 1950 participants of the International Mariological Congress that took place in Rome to celebrate the newly defined dogma of the Assumption of Mary, petitioned Pius XII to define Mary's collaboration in the redemptive work of Jesus. See Aidan Nichols, *There Is No Rose: The Mariology of the Catholic Church* (Minneapolis: Fortress Press, 2015), 80.

8. See Frederick M. Jelly, "The Theological Context of and Introduction to Chapter 8 of *Lumen Gentium*," in *Marian Studies* 37, art. 10 (1986): 44–45.

9. John Paul II, general audience, The Holy See, October 1, 1997, 3, https://www.vatican.va/content/john-paul-ii/en/audiences/1997/documents/hf_jp-ii_aud_01101997.html.

10. See the International Marian Association, *The Role of Mary in Redemption: A Document of the Theological Commission of the International Marian Association*, 2017, 2, https://internationalmarian.com/sites/marian/files/uploads/documents/the_role_of_mary_in_redemption_1.pdf.

11. See the International Marian Association, *The Role of Mary in Redemption*, 4, note 33.

12. Mark Miravalle quoted in Nichols, *There Is No Rose*, 88.

13. See also *RM*, chapter 3.

14. Pope Benedict XV, *Inter Soldalica*, AAS 10, 181–182.

15. See the International Marian Commission, *The Role of Mary in Redemption*, 3.

16. Aidan Nichols records the commentary of Justin Martyr, Irenaeus, Jerome, Ambrose, among others. St. Ambrose, in his commentary on the Gospel of Luke wrote the following, *"Perhaps indeed, knowing that by the death of her Son the redemption of the world was worked, she hoped to be able by her own death-to-herself to contribute some little to what was accomplished for the profit of all."* St. Bernard of Clairvaux and St. Thomas Aquinas commented in a similar fashion. St. Albert the Great referred to Mary as the "helpmate of the redeemer." For more detail see *There Is No Rose*, 111–31.

17. International Marian Commission, *The Role of Mary in Redemption*, 4.

18. René Laurentin, *Traite sur al Vierge Marie*, 2009, quoted in Robert Fastiggi, "Pope Francis, the Humility of Mary and the Role of Co-redemptrix," May 28, 2020, https://www.motherofallpeoples.com/post/pope-francis-the-humility-of-mary-and-the-role-of-co-redemptrix.

19. See his 2000 interview with Peter Seewald in *God and World* (San Francisco: Ignatius Press, 2000), 306. "The formula 'Co-redemptrix' departs too great an extent from the language of Scripture and of the Fathers and therefore gives rise to misunderstandings....A correct intention is being expressed the wrong way."

20. Pope Benedict XVI, homily, Solemnity of Mary, the Mother of God, December 31, 2008.

Notes

21. International Marian Association, *The Role of Mary in Redemption*, 2.

22. Edward Sri, *Walking with Mary: A Biblical Journey from Nazareth to the Cross* (New York: Image Press, 2017), 71.

23. Douay-Rheims version/translation of the Vulgate, emphasis mine.

24. For more on the influence of the Latin translation of the Bible, the Vulgate, see Jimmy Akin, "Is the Vulgate the Catholic Church's Official Bible?" *National Catholic Register*, September 5, 2017.

25. Augustine, *Christian Instruction; Admonition and Grace; The Christian Combat; Faith, Hope and Charity* (Washington, DC: Catholic University of America Press, 2002), 339.

26. Pope Francis, homily, "Our Lady of Sorrows: Disciple and Mother," The Holy See, April 3, 2020, https://www.vatican.va/content/francesco/en/cotidie/2020/documents/papa-francesco-cotidie_20200403_1-addolorata-discepola-emadre.html#:~:text=Our%20Lady%20did%20not%20want,this%20title%20cannot%20be%20duplicated.

27. Pope Francis, Message on the Feast of the Vow, May 13, 2023, http://www.arcidiocesisassari.it/2023/05/28/festa-del-voto-il-messaggio-del-santo-padre/.

28. *LG* 54, emphasis mine.

29. Pope Paul VI, Address, November 21, 1964, quoted in John Paul II, *Redemptoris Mater*, The Holy See, March 25, 1987, 47.

30. See Nichols, *There Is No Rose*, 67–88.

31. Nichols, *There Is No Rose*, 86.

32. Nichols, *There Is No Rose*, 76.

33. CDF, *Letter to the Bishops of the Catholic Church on the Collaboration of Men and Women in the Church and in the World*, May 31, 2004, 6, note 5, emphasis mine.

34. John Paul II, *Redemptoris Mater*, 11.

35. See CDF, Declaration *Inter Insigniores* [On the Question of the Admission of Women to the Ministerial Priesthood], The Holy See, October 15, 1976, https://www.vatican.va/roman_curia/congregations/cfaith/documents/rc_con_cfaith_doc_19761015_inter-insigniores_en.html.

Marian Approaches to Synodality

36. John Paul II, *Ordinatio Sacerdotalis* [On Reserving Priestly Ordination to Men Alone], The Holy See, May 22, 1994, 2, https://www.vatican.va/content/john-paul-ii/en/apost_letters/1994/documents/hf_jp-ii_apl_19940522_ordinatio-sacerdotalis.html. Cf. *LG* 20–21.

37. John Paul II, *Ordinatio Sacerdotalis*, 1.

38. John Paul II, *Ordinatio Sacerdotalis*, 3, emphasis mine.

39. See CDF, *Inter Insigniores*, 6, emphasis mine.

40. Romans 16:7 refers to Andronicus and Junia, "my relatives who were in prison with me; they are prominent among the apostles, and they were in Christ before I was." The footnote in the NRSV indicates ancient authorities read Julia. There has been some debate as to whether Junia was a woman. In chapter 3, we discovered St. Mary Magdalene's title as "Apostle to the Apostles" and St. Photine as "Equal to the Apostles." St. Faustina has been given the title "Apostle of Divine Mercy."

41. See the Pastoral Commission of the Sacred Congregation for the Evangelization of Peoples, "The Role of Women in Evangelization," 1976 in *Vatican Council II: More Post Conciliar Documents* (Northport, New York: Costello Publishing Company, 1982), 319.

42. The twelfth apostle, Matthias, replaced Judas Iscariot, and was elected after the description of this scene in the upper room. See Acts 1:26.

43. Cardinal Joseph Ratzinger and Vittorio Messori, *The Ratzinger Report. An Exclusive Interview on the State of the Church* (San Francisco: Ignatius Press, 1985), 105.

44. Emphasis mine.

www.ingramcontent.com/pod-product-compliance
Lightning Source LLC
Chambersburg PA
CBHW070551160426
43199CB00014B/2457